Infinity

Sara Bighash

ISBN: 978-1-7773078-0-6

Editor: Lee Ann at First-Editing.com

Cover Design: Bogdan Matei

Author Photo: Joe Lavee

Contents

Love

Love is the strongest force in the universe. Love is the binding glue holding everything together. Love is the supreme force that connects us to one another. Of everything we see, only love is infinite. Only love will last. Love is indescribable. Inexplicable. It can only be felt by the heart. Love is the essence of our being. Love is what we are deep within our souls. Love is unity. Love is perfection. In love, we see ourselves reflected in one another. We see ourselves in everything around us. Love takes us beyond this world. Love takes us to infinity.

Faith

Faith is absolute trust. It is trust that the universe is working for your highest good. It is trusting in the unknown. Faith is when you see the light with your heart when all your eyes see is darkness. It's synonymous to walking through a dark tunnel and taking out a flashlight. It's seeing just that one ray of light ahead of you. It's that spark of hope inside your heart that keeps you going. Faith is knowing that you are being divinely guided. It's seeing the good in each seemingly bad situation. It's seeing beyond appearances and looking at the wisdom hidden within each situation. It is knowing that there is purpose to everything, and nothing happens by chance. Faith is knowing that you are divinely protected by an unseen force; the Source from which everything comes. Something greater than us is always guiding and protecting us. We may not be able to see it with our eyes, but we can feel it deep within our being. Faith is knowing in our hearts that the universe is always guiding us from above.

Peace

Peace comes from within. It cannot be obtained externally. It's a completely internal process. We can't reach peace by achieving something, by reaching a certain status, or by gaining possessions. We can't look for it in objects or circumstances. The only place peace can be found is within. Only by shifting our attention inwardly can we find peace. Only by drowning out the noise of our own mind do we feel it. By going into stillness, we find that peace is always with us. Often, we believe that we must change a situation to feel at peace. But if we want peace, it is with us immediately. It is always found in the present moment, in the here and now. When we offer no resistance to what is, when we allow this moment to be, without covering it up with mental noise, we are at peace. We cannot make it into a future goal or a destination. Peace is always available to us. We must only work to remove the barriers and look within our hearts. By seeing through our grief, anger, and despair, and finding the stillness underneath, we find peace. By allowing every emotion that we feel to be, we feel at peace. Sometimes, in the most difficult circumstances, we feel peace from within through grace.

Gratitude

We've all heard of the power of gratitude, but we often don't grasp its depth. We often don't fully understand its power. Gratitude is not only a practice, it's also a state of being. It's a shift in perspective. It's when we raise our level of awareness and notice the little things in life. It's when we become aware of how life is working in our favor, opening doors for us and nudging us in the right direction. It's when we pay attention to all the little miracles that have happened in our lives and all the ways that life is supporting us. It's noticing all the times we were saved from misfortune by grace. It's noticing that life is always helping us evolve and grow. It's noticing all the guides that life sends us in the form of people and circumstances. Gratitude is when we pay attention to the wonders of life. It's when we feel one with life. Open your heart and notice all the good around you. Notice the beauty of life itself.

Passion

Whatever it is that you feel naturally drawn to, whatever brings joy to your heart, go after it with your whole being because that is your soul's path. Whatever it is that creates a spark in your soul, seek it wholeheartedly. Allow yourself to be pulled by that passion. Allow it to draw you in closer. You know deep down that it resonates with your heart and soul. When you do something with your entire being, there's a whole different energy that flows through you. You are fully present, and you feel the energy field of your own being. You feel vibrant and ecstatic. You feel connected. It is inevitable that when you do something with a deep sense of joy, you will achieve mastery. You become an artist, an architect. You become one with the activity. Go after what your heart desires. Let passion ignite your spirit.

Fulfillment

As human beings, we all want to feel fulfilled. But fulfillment doesn't come from what we achieve or what we get. It comes from who we become and what we can give. Fulfillment comes from growing into stronger versions of ourselves. Fulfillment comes from our growth and how deeply we can impact other people in a positive way. It's about how much love and joy we can bring to other people's hearts. Fulfillment is about achieving excellence within ourselves so we can add value to other people. When we grow our own potential and use it to benefit others, we feel fulfilled. Fulfillment comes from living our truth and sharing our heart and spirit with others. Fulfillment comes from living deep in the heart.

Paradoxes

In life, we often learn what joy is through first experiencing pain and suffering. We learn to seek the light by going through the darkness. We learn to value and appreciate the presence of others through their absence. We come to be grateful for what we have when we experience having little. When confronted with difficult circumstances, we have to fully accept what is before the situation changes or before we can act. In life, we often have to lose ourselves completely in order to discover who we really are. We often have to go into a place of not knowing for answers to come to us. In life, we must often let go of expectation for everything to come to us. In life, we must often give in order to get. These are the paradoxes of life. Look deeply within these paradoxes and feel the profound truth that lies within them.

See Through Appearances

When confronted with a situation, don't look at the situation itself. Look at what lies beyond it. When answering a question, don't look at the question itself. Look at what lies behind the question. Seek to understand where the question is coming from. Look beyond the words being said. When confronted with a challenge, don't look at the difficulty. Look at the secret lesson it's trying to teach you. Look at the hidden message encoded within the situation. Open your eyes to what the universe is trying to show you. When a door is closed, don't go into despair. Look at the opportunities the closed door has allowed to open for you. Look at how it has forced you to change the direction of your gaze and see other doors you didn't see before. Look at new opportunities being presented to you in the face of a lost one. When you are in a seemingly negative circumstance, look for the good hidden in it. Look for the good that lies beyond appearances. Beyond what you are able to perceive. Beyond what the mind can understand. Only then will you be able to see truth. Only then will you find the hidden messages.

Forgiveness

Forgiveness is one of the most powerful acts there is. To forgive means to see through a person's flaws and mistakes. It means seeing through faults and looking at the human being underneath. Forgiveness is a vital part of our spiritual growth and healing. We must not only forgive others, but also ourselves. We must treat ourselves and others with grace and compassion. With forgiveness comes great power. When you forgive someone, you automatically feel a release within yourself. The situation loses its weight and your energy is no longer consumed by anger and grief. Through forgiveness, you can redirect your attention towards the things you love. This is the true magic of forgiveness.

Forgiveness is not something that happens on the outside. It's a process that happens within. When you forgive someone, you can feel internally that you have been freed. You can feel there is no longer resistance within you. You feel at one with life again. You feel your energy flowing again. This is the true power of forgiveness. All we have to do is take the lessons, become a little wiser, and move forward. Through forgiveness, we find our greatest strength. By forgiving ourselves and others, we live in a state of grace. We live with peace in our hearts.

More to Life

Have you ever thought to yourself: There has to be more to life? More than the routine, more than simply going along with everything. Have you ever felt your soul wanting to break free? Have you ever felt a powerful energy throbbing in your soul, telling you it wants more? Have you ever felt the desire deep within to accomplish something extraordinary? If you've ever felt that desire, it's not just because you want to do something new. It's because deep down, you want to *become someone new*. You want to expand. You want to become spontaneous and take risks. You want to become someone who goes after what they truly want; someone who's not afraid of rejection. Someone who's not afraid of failure. *That* is the person you want to become. If you've ever felt that burning desire light up your soul like a candle, then you are ready. So be courageous. Step out of your comfort zone because on the other side, that's when life truly begins. That's where the hidden secrets are. That's where you will find your true self. It's where you will discover your true potential. Step forward and don't look back. Just trust.

Living Authentically

Living authentically means living our truth. It means showing who we are in our innermost being. It means living by our own standards and our own values. It means not seeking anyone's approval in our life direction, other than our own. It means going after what we truly want with our heart and soul. When we live authentically, we no longer concern ourselves with the opinion of others. We are not swayed by flattery or criticism. We don't worry about the perception of others; we view ourselves by our own standards. We don't compare ourselves to others; we seek to better ourselves. When we live authentically, we live deeper in our spirit. We seek joy from within, not without. We seek only to be ourselves, letting go of worry and self-judgement. We go after what we want without fear of reprisal. Living authentically means living freely.

Becoming Selective

As we grow on our spiritual journey, we become more selective. We become more intentional with what we dedicate our time and energy to. We become more selective in who we share our presence with. We start realizing that a meaningful life is one lived with intention and awareness. We come to truly value ourselves and realize that our presence, our being, is the most precious gift we can share with anyone. We start realizing that even though there are many options along our path, we have to choose the ones that resonate with our soul. We realize that we don't have to try every opportunity we find, but only seek those that are representative of who we are and that will help us grow. By being intentional, we dedicate our time and energy to things that truly matter to us. By being selective, we are careful who we share our time with. We surround ourselves with those who support our growth and celebrate our successes. We start to share our energy with those who have good intentions for us and live in the heart. By becoming selective, we live authentically and make choices that are in alignment with our higher self.

Longing to be Heard

All of us have a longing, deep down, to be heard. All of us long for the feeling of being understood. We each wish for another soul to hear us, to know what is in our heart; a soul that will see the depth of our being. A soul that will truly see who we are. Though on the surface it may seem that some people only want attention or shallow friendships, deep down, they too long to be heard. Beneath the veil, behind appearances, their hearts long to be understood. They may be afraid of sharing what is in their heart and may hint at it indirectly, hoping someone will catch on, looking for someone who will understand. Each of us holds so many things in our heart. All we want is for someone to understand. All we want is to be heard. Perhaps today, you can be a listener. Perhaps today, you will hear someone's soul and fill that longing in them. You can be that soul someone opens up to. You can be the deep listener someone else is seeking.

Deep Listening

When someone comes pouring their heart out to you, practice silence. When someone is telling you their story, learn to be still. When someone is sharing their joy, their sorrows, their dreams, their pains, simply listen to them. Be patient as a rock. Give them your undivided attention, for the most valuable thing you can give to anyone is your attention and your presence. Allow them to express their soul without being interrupted, without them getting a sense that you may be thinking of a response. Simply allow them to be. Show that you are present. Let them know you are completely with them. Feel the energy field as they speak. Allow yourself to feel your own soul, your inner being, while they speak to you so you may relate not necessarily to their words or the storyline, but to the human being underneath it. This level of connection is so much deeper.

At the same time, hear what they are saying. Come from a place of understanding. Do not criticize, judge, or put labels on them. Simply understand. It can be tempting to try and formulate a response while someone is speaking, but practice holding back. Deep listening can work miracles.

Appreciation

We don't often realize this, but when we seek out and appreciate the good in others, we are making magic. By paying attention to and pointing out the good in others, we create a spark in them. We reflect their own goodness back to them. We seek out the seeds of positivity within others and water them.

True appreciation shouldn't be confused with flattery. Appreciation is genuine praise that comes from the heart. It's noticing the good intent and acts of kindness. Whenever we notice something and give it attention, we are giving it energy and allowing it to grow. When we see the good in others, we are also developing that goodness in ourselves. When we seek out other people's good qualities—their gentleness, their compassion, their sincerity, their kind-heartedness—we are also seeking out those qualities within ourselves. By nurturing the seeds of positivity in others, we are nurturing positivity within ourselves. Other people are mirrors, and we see ourselves reflected in them. By uplifting others, we are essentially uplifting ourselves.

Intention

Intention is everything. Someone you just met can have better intentions for you than someone you've known for a lifetime. At first, this realization may come across as a sad truth. But in reality, it's a relief. Knowing this is liberating. It means that at any point in your life, there's a chance you'll meet someone who has the best intentions for you. On any given day, someone can enter your life who will have the intent of bringing love, friendship, and joy into your life.

We don't necessarily have to hold onto everyone from our past simply because we've known them for so long. We don't have to maintain friendships if they are no longer serving our higher good. There's no need to become dependent on people simply because of attachments. We don't have to become stagnant. We don't have to settle. There's always room for new people to enter our lives.

There will always be people out there who have good intentions for us; people that will help us grow. We just have to keep our hearts open. Time is not everything. Intention is everything. It is far more valuable than time. What lies in a person's heart is what truly matters.

Alchemist

In the hermetic tradition, an alchemist is one who has mastered the art of turning base metal into gold. In the beginning of our spiritual journey, we might find it difficult to overcome obstacles and turn negative experiences into positive ones. But as we grow and develop on our path, this task becomes easier for us. We become alchemists in our own lives. We gain the ability to turn our deepest pains into joy. We can take any negativity along our path and turn it into positivity. This is the real secret to life—to learn to respond to difficult situations with patience rather than frustration. To respond to bitterness with kindness. To allow the pains that have hardened our hearts to crack open the shell of the ego and let our soul, our true nature, emerge. To allow our pains to make us softer and more compassionate.

To be an alchemist means to flow with life; to resist nothing. To be an alchemist means to find the good that is hidden within every situation. It is looking beyond duality and trusting the universal intelligence. By becoming an alchemist, we dissolve negative energy along our path and turn it into positive vibration.

Evolving

As we evolve into our higher selves, we notice that the energies that no longer serve us start to dissipate. We notice a shift in what we pay attention to and what we don't. We become selective in what we dedicate our time and energy to. Slowly, things that were holding us back start to drift away. It's as if the universe removes them for us. The universe cleanses our lives and makes space for better things to come. By letting go of old ways of thinking that do not serve us, we allow for better things to enter our lives. By letting go of old energies, we let new energy in. As we evolve to higher states of consciousness, everything around us changes.

Power

Each one of us has ultimate power in our own lives. We have the power to achieve anything in life we set out to. We have the power to alter our perception. We have the power to take a different approach to what we're doing. We have the power to shift our focus to what is truly important to us; to what we value most. We have the power to turn our eyes to our goals and put all our energy into working towards them.

Once we recognize this truth—once we realize we have the power to do anything in our lives we want to do—this truth will shape our life. Our true power starts to emerge. Our true capabilities begin to surface and we see the potential we were holding all along. We see that nothing is too big to reach. No dream is too far-fetched.

With the realization that the power is within us, miracles start to happen. We notice that where we put our energy gives results. The more we believe in ourselves, the more we can achieve. The more we move towards our goals, the more they seem to be coming towards us. Discover your inner power and allow it to emerge. Manifest the reality you desire.

Inner Capacities

Look for your inner capacities, your inner strength. Look for the power you hold within. Don't lose yourself in outside circumstances. Know that circumstances are not stable—everything is bound to change. Challenges will always be there, but the nature of these challenges and the way in which you approach them varies. Turn inward. Keep an internal locus of control. Know that you have the capacity to achieve whatever you set out to achieve. Know that there is an energy source deep within your soul. Remain grounded and focused. Keep your attention on your goals, on what it is you wish to accomplish. Know that your inner capacities will guide you and show you the way.

Listen to your inner voice. Use your inner power. Know that you have the strength to overcome any adversity you may face. Know that you are being divinely guided. Know that you have a higher purpose. Whatever you want in this world is inside of you. Don't look outside. Look within.

Butterfly Effect

Do you know how powerful you are? Do you have any idea what you are capable of? Every word you speak and every action you take has a ripple effect. Everything you say and do sends a vibrational ripple across the universe. Your words and actions impact not only the people you are directly interacting with, but also those you don't even know. With your words, with your gestures, you can change someone's internal state, and the impact affects how that individual interacts with others.

There is a domino effect to your words and actions. You have the ability to uplift other souls with your kind words and gestures and in doing so, you indirectly affect many more whom you've never met. The effect of your words and actions go beyond your own perception. Never underestimate the impact you have. Never underestimate the power of kind words and gestures. Know that positivity is contagious. Use your power to spread love and positivity all around you. Flap your wings and change the world through the butterfly effect.

Communicating

So often, we think the people around us must know how we feel. So often, we believe it is others' responsibility to detect our emotions and our needs. What we don't realize is, without communication, it is impossible for others to know how we feel deep down or what it is we want.

Communication is so vital in our interactions and in our relationships. Most of the time, we cannot intuitively know what a person is thinking or how they're feeling. It is so important to explain how we feel. It is vital that we develop clear channels of communication with those close to us by expressing our thoughts and practicing deep listening. By doing so, we create mutual trust and understanding. We clear assumptions and misunderstandings. We dissolve negativity.

Through clear communication, we can let one another know how we've interpreted a conversation, a situation, or an event. We speak our truth when we feel misunderstood or not heard. We begin to heal relationships and bring positivity into our interactions. Conflicts dissolve and bonds strengthen. Communication is vital for our own well-being and for our relationships.

Understanding

We must always strive to understand people instead of judging. There is a big difference when we approach people's ideas, beliefs, words, and actions from a place of understanding rather than a place of judgement. It changes the way we look at things. It allows us to adopt the other person's lens and see things from their point of view. It allows us to learn something new and to mold our own belief system to fit in new information. It allows us to adapt.

Understanding allows us to see where the other person is coming from. It allows us to see our own biases and beliefs. Although it is tempting to judge someone whose beliefs are not in alignment with ours, by judging, we only limit ourselves. By judging, we put up walls. Through understanding, we break down the ego. We break down the illusion of separation and see ourselves as one with everyone else. Through understanding, there is love and compassion. Only through putting ourselves into other people's shoes and trying to understand them can we truly connect with other human beings.

Healer of Hearts

Become a healer of hearts. Walk out of your house like a shepherd. Help someone's soul heal. Give those around you wings to fly. Become a magician and sprinkle them with the magic of sweet words and kind deeds. See the best in people and allow it to surface. Help people see the good qualities they hold that they may not be aware of.

When you meet people who are in despair, sit beside them. Instill hope in their hearts simply with your presence. When you are at peace and hold good intentions, your being becomes so powerful that it heals those around you. You become radiant and carry the light with you wherever you go. When someone comes to you longing for kindness, soothe their heart with kind words. In every situation you find yourself in, ask yourself: How can I be of help here? How can I give my all? Always seek to add value to other people, to enrich their lives with goodness and loving-kindness. Feel your connectedness with everyone else. Know that what you do to others, you do to yourself. Do good for others. It will come back in unexpected ways.

Power of Language

Language is an art that needs to be mastered. There is hidden power in the words we speak, the tone of our voice, and our gestures. Our words can make someone feel loved or they can make someone feel empty. They can leave someone feeling empowered, or they can leave them feeling discouraged. They can cause sparks of hope to go off inside a person's heart, or they can leave that person feeling destitute. They can cause the light of inspiration to ignite in someone's soul, or they can extinguish the flames that were already there.

With our words, we have the power to make someone's heart sink. We also have the power to infuse another person with love, hope, and appreciation. We can make someone recognize the love and light they hold within. We can make others believe in their own capabilities.

There is great power in words. Infuse kind words into the sentences you speak. Integrate love into your everyday language. Bring kindness and compassion into every conversation you have. Dare to sprinkle other people with the magic of the kind words that come from your heart. Use the power of language to instill love and positivity in other people's hearts.

Your Life

Look carefully around you and notice that life is always happening. Life is always moving. As you walk outside, pay attention to the sound of cars passing by. Notice the people walking past you to get to their destination. Feel the vibrancy of life. Feel the aliveness of everything around you. Feel the energy of life itself. Recognize that your life is always unfolding in this moment. Realize that your life is always happening in the now. Life is energy in motion.

Never confuse your life with your life situation. Your life situation consists of a set of circumstances the mind judges as good or bad. Your life, on the other hand, is the perfection in this moment. It is the joy in this moment that is beyond the mind. Your life is the pure bliss of being. Watch the miracle of life unfold all around you. Feel the pure joy of life itself.

.

Free Yourself

Free yourself from the constraints of society. Free yourself from ideas of right and wrong. Free yourself from all the shoulds and shouldn'ts. Know that life was never meant to be confining or restraining. Know that life was designed to be limitless. Know that you are an infinite being and there are no limits, no boundaries, to who you are or what you can achieve. You are not confined by anything; not by social standards or any belief system.

None of these define you. Because to define something means to limit it; to put it in a box. You are as vast as the universe itself. You are so much more than you know. Allow yourself to be who you are at the core of your being. Liberate yourself from whatever is holding you back. Let go of ideology. Let go of definitions. Let go of all mental abstracts. Let go of all ideas you have about yourself until you only feel your pure essence. Free yourself. Liberate your soul. Break free.

Focus

When you have a goal, focus on it. Give it your undivided attention. Once you know what it is you wish to achieve, go after it with your whole heart and soul. Don't let fear or inconsistency crawl in. Guard your focus. Become the gatekeeper of your awareness, not letting in any trespassers. Hold onto your vision, your dream. Close your eyes and imagine your dream. Feel it with your heart. Allow your focus to guide you. Allow all your energy to flow towards that goal, what it is that you can see with your mind's eye. Know that imagination is the creative faculty of the mind. It has the power to bring things into existence.

Don't allow yourself to let go of the strong pull of your vision. Hold onto it and let it guide you to your dreams. You just have to keep believing and trusting. When you are working towards your goal, give it your all. Be fully present. Then watch the miracles unfold. Keep your vision and your focus clear. Be patient. Be persistent. Manifest your dreams.

Invest in Yourself

Invest in yourself. Take time for yourself to develop your strengths and abilities. Take time to go inward and reflect. Discover your hidden potential; your talents and abilities. Recognize your ability to manifest your dreams, to bring joy and beauty into this world. You are powerful beyond words. Recognize your own power. Find that place in your heart that is aching to show its creativity. Find that place in your soul that is longing for expression. Use your potential, your abilities, to manifest your dreams. Use your potential to express what is deep within your soul. Invest in your own growth and uncover everything you are, deep within your being.

Your Divine Nature

Always remember your true nature—your divinity. You were made perfect, reflecting the perfection of the Creator. You reflect divine beauty. You bring into this world the light from the Unmanifest. Your soul is transparent to the light of consciousness that comes from beyond. You carry within you the essence of the world beyond. You are the universe becoming aware of itself. You are one with the Source of all existence.

With your light, with your heart, you can make magic happen. With the love you carry within you, the love that is the root of your very being, you bring beauty into this world. Use the light in your heart to light the candle in other people's hearts. The fire in your heart can light up the whole world. You are love. You are divine.

Masterpiece

Each one of us is our own masterpiece. We are creating ourselves in every moment. We are constantly changing, constantly evolving. In each moment, we're making a choice. We are choosing who we want to be. We're choosing what to create out of that moment. We bring things into existence by the choices we make.

Each decision we make builds who we are. We are like art pieces that are always in the process of being created. We are like sculptures always being shaped. We have the power to design ourselves the way we want. We are indeed our own masterpiece. The thoughts we have, the emotions we feel, the things we do, are all part of the creative process.

Even in circumstances that are beyond our control, we are still making a choice. We choose how to react to each situation. We have this profound capacity to take a situation and make the best of it. Each moment can be a new opportunity. Each moment can be an opening for something new to emerge.

The joy we bring into the activities we do is our choice. The energy we put into the things we love is our choice. We choose what we dedicate our time and energy to. We choose where to focus our attention. And with everything we do, whether it is a thought or an action, we are in the process of creation. We are artists, creating the masterpiece of who we are.

Fear vs Love

In spirituality, it is said that we always act out of either two states: fear, or love. So many of us don't go after our dreams because we're afraid of facing failure. So often, we don't chase the desires of our hearts simply because we don't know if we will make it. We start having doubts and thinking, *What if I'm not good enough? What if this doesn't work out?* Neither of these thoughts has a basis in reality. They are only thoughts. If you've ever looked closely at individuals who've achieved success, you will see that they went after their dreams without a spark of fear. They operated out of love. They had faith in their heart and saw only the light. They had a vision and they went after it with their entire being. They channeled an energy from within to reach their dreams and desires.

Look inside you. Recognize your potential; your strengths and your creative abilities. Find out what lies in your heart. Go after what it is you are naturally drawn to. Go after what sets your soul on fire. Don't be afraid of failure. Know that feeling the joy of going after what you want is already success. When you do what you love in life, you have already succeeded. Know that operating out of fearlessness, out of love, will ignite a fire within you that cannot be contained. Know that if you take the first step with faith, the rest will follow. Your heart will guide you.

The Test

When we're faced with difficult circumstances—when we're given challenges that seem almost impossible to deal with—we have to keep in mind, these are the tests. The obstacles don't block the path. The obstacles *are* the path. The issue isn't the problems we face. It's that we think we're not supposed to have them. But the reality is, the barriers we face call us to our higher selves. They help us evolve on our spiritual path. They often force us to generate powers that we didn't know we had.

A life without hardship, a life without challenges, would be an empty life. It would be deprived of any real meaning. It's through challenges that we uncover our greatest strengths. It's through difficulties that we gain invaluable life skills. It's how we learn to persevere. It's often in times of hardship that we come to know who we want to be; it's when we obtain the power of self-mastery. We have to keep our eyes open and pay attention to what each situation is teaching us.

Spark of Hope

There may be times when we feel like we've hit rock bottom. Times when we feel destitute. But it's during our hardest times that we find a spark of hope. It's like we're in the darkness and we see a shooting star flashing across the night sky. We feel a candle light up within our spirit. We sense it in our hearts. Just one ray of hope is enough to show us there's a way out of the darkness. Just one ray is enough to light our spirit and bring peace to our hearts.

In times of great difficulty, we have to look for that spark within us. We have to look deep within our spirit. We have to look within our hearts and see the light beyond the darkness. We have to open our heart and let hope ignite the candle of our spirit. There's always a spark of hope somewhere. We just have to find it.

Healing Ourselves

In healing ourselves, we become healers of others. We heal the planet. There is no work more sacred than this. Healing ourselves means clearing our energy field from negativity. It means letting go of any thought, emotion, or action that doesn't serve us. It means dissolving the past by becoming fully present. It means becoming the gatekeeper of our mind and noticing where our attention drifts off to. It means stepping out of the dream of thinking so we are not trapped by repetitive mind patterns.

When we heal ourselves, we start living in the present. We start cherishing every moment. When we heal our own thoughts and emotions, we change our life. We change our entire being and respond differently to every situation and every person around us. When we heal ourselves, we act out of present-moment awareness and know what to do when a situation requires us to act immediately. We know how to respond to the demands of the present moment.

When someone asks for words of wisdom, the right words come through us. We instinctively know what the person needs. We become aligned, and the right tools come our way in the right moment. We find solutions to the obstacles we face. When we heal ourselves, we become a healing force for others.

Surrender

Sometimes when we are going through a hard time, we feel the need to control the situation. We feel the need to exert power and resist what is happening. But there are times when we cannot do much on the outer level. There are times when trying to change the situation is counterproductive.

Sometimes, the greatest thing we can do is let the situation be. Sometimes, the most powerful thing we can do is surrender. Surrender is when we completely accept what is and make peace with it. On the surface, it may appear like weakness. But on a deeper level, it is an act of great power. It's when we become transparent to the situation and the situation no longer has power over us. It loses its grip and we are no longer at the mercy of what happens on the outside because we are no longer reacting.

Sometimes surrender happens automatically. Sometimes, when we find ourselves in an extremely difficult situation, we quickly realize that we have no choice but to fully accept what is—and an internal shift happens. We are suddenly at peace. When we let go of the illusion of control, our true power emerges. Whatever circumstance you find yourself in, don't resist it. Merge with it and allow life to flow through you. Peace lies in surrendering to what is.

Grace

You are a river. Grace is an ocean. Merge with the ocean of grace and let it take you into stillness. Give up to grace and allow it to take you into peace. Allow it to clear your mind and heart. Let it renew your spirit. Let it heal you. Let it take away the heaviness of your heart. Let it melt away your troubles in ways you didn't know were possible. Allow it to restore your soul and shower you with divine love. Let it sweep away the old and bring new energy to your life. Give up resistance to what is. Give up resistance to life and let the serenity of grace take you over.

Patience

Nothing great can be achieved without patience. It is so vital, so crucial in life. Patience is a powerful tool. It is an art that needs to be mastered. So often in life we go after something, but our own impatience causes us to give up before we've reached our goal. Sometimes we get so caught up in achieving our goal that our steps become no more than a means to an end. Sometimes we get so caught up in arriving that we miss the journey. We forget to enjoy the process and cherish the moment.

When we don't honor the present moment, resistance and negativity arise. We have to learn to live completely in the now and give our full attention to the step we are taking. Whatever goal we have or whatever it is we wish to achieve, we have to practice patience. We have to allow time for our actions to bear fruit. We have to be careful not to project ourselves into the future. Instead of asking *what's next?* We should always ask *what's here?* Within each step we take lies concealed lessons and secrets from the universe. We have to look deeply into where we are and honor each step of our path. We have to master the art of patience.

In the Same Boat

It's funny how we're often afraid of talking about our problems, yet there are usually people around us going through the same thing. Sometimes there are things we don't want to reveal because we're afraid of being judged; afraid of being looked at differently. But the irony is that sometimes the person we're afraid to confide in is dealing with the same issue.

There are so many challenges people face but never talk about. So many things we keep in our hearts because we don't know what will happen if we let them out. Sometimes the challenges we're confronted with seem beyond what we think we can handle. So often, we're faced with these challenges without warning. But surely, we're not alone. There's always someone out there who has gone through the same thing; someone who knows what it's like. And even though it seems hard, even though it may feel like we're jeopardizing our image, sometimes letting a friend know about what we're going through can change everything. It often makes the challenge lose its weight. Sometimes opening up to someone we trust can make all the difference. It allows a new door to open. It allows us to hear another person's story and gain perspective. It can break the taboo of the problem itself and we no longer feel trapped inside a box. We realize that often, we're in the same boat as someone close to us.

Acting out of Love

Have you ever noticed that when you act out of love, your action has a certain quality to it? Have you noticed the nice, tingly feeling that comes with it? When we do something out of a feeling of love, there's an inherently positive quality attached to it. When we do something out of love, both the action and the reward bring us joy and we feel the positivity grow within us. We feel aligned when we act out of love. We feel one with life.

Truly then, this is the purpose of life: To do everything out of love. To bring love into everything we do. Whatever it is we're after, whatever it is we wish to manifest, we have to see what feeling lies behind it. We have to check where our intention is coming from. Do we wish to achieve something because we feel obliged to, or because we truly want to? Are we going after something to impress others, or because it's our heart's desire?

When we make decisions out of love, when we act out of love, we feel intrinsically happy. Our actions are then not just a means to an end; our actions become an end in and of themselves. And that is so beautiful, so powerful, so rewarding. Anything that is done out of love feels liberating.

Abundance

Abundance is all around us, if only we pay attention to it; if only we open our hearts. As you walk through life, feel the abundance all around you. Feel the fullness of life itself. Feel the energy of the sun, the lightness of the air, and the softness of water. Feel the ground you are walking on and realize that it is supporting all life forms. It is supporting life itself. All of these elements are working together in harmony to make life possible for us here on earth. They are always giving in abundance.

Recognize the abundance in human relationships. Recognize the love that is shared between people; between family members, friends, and even strangers. Recognize the love that is shared between humans and other life forms. Recognize life's abundance in a smile, a hug, a kind gesture. Feel the fullness of life in the sun, the sky, the clouds, the trees, the different life forms, and the changing of the seasons. Recognize that life is so giving, so generous. Recognize you have within you the same life force as every other being. Recognize the source of existence within yourself. Realize that you are the source of abundance. Recognize the light and love within your heart. Feel your oneness with all of life on an energetic level. Feel the abundance from within.

Natural Communicators

Some people are natural communicators. Connecting with people comes easily to them. They have a way with words. They just know what to say in the moment. They know how to handle the situation. When you see them, you know they're being genuine. The words they speak are not just words. It comes from deep within their being. They speak their hearts. They really listen to the other individual. They become so focused on what the other person is saying that everything else becomes background noise. When they dedicate their full attention to someone, that person can feel it too. They know they're being listened to. They know they're being heard.

These natural communicators don't just listen; they also read between the lines. They get the essence of the message they're hearing. They uncover the bits and pieces of information that are not explicitly stated in the conversation. They find missing pieces of the puzzle and respond based on the underlying message. They act out of present-moment awareness. They are natural empaths. With their deeper understanding and natural ability to connect with others, they make magic happen. They allow other people to open up. They let people release the energies they're carrying in their aura. Natural communicators have a certain gift.

Talents

We each have our own talents—unique abilities we are given by nature; potential that is at the core of our being. We must find out what these talents are so they can surface. We have to look for our natural gifts and nurture them.

Sometimes we already know what we are good at, what we are drawn to. Sometimes we discover our talents coincidentally, by trying something new. No matter how we come to know our talents, we have to seek them and allow them to emerge. Strengthening our natural abilities will bring us into a state of flow with life. It will bring us deep joy. By doing what we are naturally good at, by using our talents, we live in spirit. We live in harmony. We live in sync with life.

It is up to us to discover our talents, to listen to our soul. It is up to us to develop what we are naturally good at, what resides at the core of our being. We must acknowledge and honor our individual and unique talents. By sharing our talents, we not only benefit ourselves, but also others. We can use our abilities to enhance other people's lives. Each one of us is unique. Each of us has hidden potential.

Changes

Have you ever noticed how things are always changing? Things are constantly taking a turn. As old doors close, new ones open. The seasons change, bringing with them new energy. Life is in constant motion. If you look closely, you will realize that every situation is impermanent. Nothing is as stable and solid as we may think. The only thing that is stable is our inner being. Our soul. Our inner self. The life force within us is the one thing that remains constant.

It is the same force that flows through all beings. It is the same force that is keeping the universe in motion and keeps the earth spinning. Yet everything else is in a constant cycle of creation and recreation. Old energy is being cleared as new energy emerges. New opportunities arise as old ones serve their purpose. Everything moves through the cycle of life. It grows, reaches a peak, retracts, and then a new cycle begins.

This impermanence makes life so beautiful. Just as the seasons change, so too do our lives. Just as the color of leaves change, so too do our life circumstances. Everything in nature is teaching us the impermanence of all things. It is teaching us not to attach ourselves to anything, nor be disheartened by adversity. It is telling us to enjoy every moment because every part of the journey is precious. Each stage has a purpose.

It is beautiful to know that things are always changing. New experiences, new circumstances, new chances always lie ahead. There are so many opportunities in life. There is so much more to life than we think. Change is beautiful. Allow it to flow through your life.

Inspiration

Could it be that the inspiration you seek is already inside you? Could it be that everything you are looking for is already within you? There is a spark deep within your soul, a light that ignites your spirit. This light draws you to your greatest desires. It's the light that goes off every time you get a glimpse of all the possibilities. It goes off each time you discover your own abilities. It's the magnetic pull within you that draws you towards what you truly want. It's an inner knowing telling you that you can manifest your dreams.

To be inspired means to live in spirit. It means to follow your spirit and walk on the path that brings you deep joy. Look within yourself. The inspiration you seek is already there.

Heaven on Earth

Heaven is not a place up in the sky. Heaven is a place on earth. We create it. We manifest it. We bring it into existence. Do you know how we create heaven on earth? With the power of love. When we love to our highest capacity, when we give our all in whatever we do—that's when we are in heaven. When we show our love to those around us without reluctance, without hesitation—that is when we feel serenity. When we bring loving energy into whatever we do, we feel pure bliss. When we fearlessly pursue our dreams and operate from a state of love, we feel joy.

By showing love and kindness towards others and pursuing our dreams with heart and soul, we create heaven here on earth. Wherever you are and whatever you do, operate from a place of love. Feel its vibration within your heart. Embody the energy of love and create heaven on earth.

Beauty

Our beauty comes from within us. It comes from deep within our soul. Our beauty comes from the gentleness of our hearts. It lies within the kind words we speak and the good we do for others. Our beauty is in our pure intentions for others. When we lend someone a helping hand, there is beauty. When we uplift someone's spirit, there is beauty. When we operate out of love and compassion, there is beauty. We show our beauty through our kind words and gestures. The only lasting beauty is the beauty of the heart.

Simplicity

Have you ever noticed that the best things in life are the simplest? The silence in the early morning, the breeze at dawn, the sunshine, the night sky. These are the most beautiful things in life. If we pay attention, we'll notice that the greatest moments in life are those of a smile, a hug, laughter, a conversation with an old friend. When we look back, we remember the helpful gesture of others, the smile of a stranger, and the random acts of kindness. Sometimes all we want is to go outside at night and look at the stars. Sometimes all we want is to go out into nature and let it take us into stillness. It's the simple things in life that the soul craves. It's the simple things that make life profound. In simplicity, there is beauty.

Playground

This life is a playground. Go out and explore all that life has to offer. Go out and discover its hidden depth. Go out and uncover the mysteries of life. Immerse yourself in the game of life and have fun with it. Enjoy it. Realize that life is meant to be joyful. Feel the joy of life from your innermost being. See life through the eyes of a child. Live life with the spirit of a child. Live lightheartedly. Don't take yourself—or life—too seriously. Don't take things to heart or carry unnecessary baggage. Don't attach yourself to anything. Enjoy the game of life. Don't be disheartened if you fall down. Simply get back up and continue to play. Life is an adventure.

Behind the Scenes

Have you ever gotten to a point in your life where you felt that everything happened as it should have? That everything was meant to be? It's as if behind the scenes, life always knew what it was doing. It always knew how to guide you. It's as if it knew what experiences you needed for the evolution of your consciousness. It's as if, even in your hardest times, life took you down under just so you could rise up higher.

It's like life has been choreographing people and circumstances so you could be where you are today. It's as if everything was meant to happen the way it did. Every situation you were in, every decision you ever made, taught you something. There was a hidden message in all of your experiences. A deeper meaning.

Life is good at guiding us. It's good at showing us where to look. Life is very clever. It knows how to steer us in the right direction. It knows what people and circumstances we need along our path. Life puts the right tools at our disposal so we may use them to achieve our goals. Life has a way of redirecting us to the path that's best for us; the path that will help us fulfil our soul's purpose. The path in which we can give our all.

Life is very intelligent. It's always working in clever ways behind the scenes. We need only open our hearts to life and pay attention to its guidance.

Emotions

When an emotion arises, feel it completely. Don't resist it. Don't brush it off as if it were insignificant. Don't make yourself blind to it. Fully acknowledge that it's there. Feel it with your whole being. Go deeper into it. Feel it fully, but don't lose yourself in it. When you allow the emotion to be, it loses its weight. But if you resist it, it will lurk right around the corner.

Don't allow an emotion to sit within you. Otherwise, it will stay in your aura and weigh you down. When you allow the emotion to be, when you welcome it, you create space for it to be released. By practicing non-resistance, you find peace even in the most undesirable emotion. You find comfort within the discomfort. You allow each emotion to arise and then dissolve. You know that each emotion is temporary and is not who you are deep down.

Learn to sit comfortably with the emotions that arise within you. Acknowledge and honor each emotion and then release it.

Universal Guidance

Have you ever felt like the universe was supporting you? Have you ever felt in your heart that you were being divinely guided? When we open our eyes to the wonders around us, we notice that everything is talking to us. Everything around us is showing us something. Everything is our guide. If we pay attention, the universe is always communicating with us through people and circumstances, through books we read and songs we listen to—even through conversations that strangers are having as we walk by them.

We start to notice the synchronicities that happen all around us. We start noticing messages from the divine. We realize that we are constantly receiving answers to our questions. We see divinity in everything. When we come into alignment, we notice how energy is always moving to create circumstances in our favor and giving us omens to guide us along our path. When we tune into the universal frequency, we become synchronized with the rhythm of life. The universe is on our side, always guiding us from beyond.

Thoughts

Thoughts are energy. Thoughts are vibrations. Each thought holds a certain frequency. With our thoughts, we create our world. With our thoughts, we manifest our reality. Everything that has ben created originated in thought. Everything is created twice; first in the mind, and then in reality. With the great power we have to create with our thoughts, we have to be very careful. We have to be mindful of what we are thinking in each moment. We must take care not to dwell on the past or sink into negativity. We have to be the gatekeepers of our minds. Always watching. Always alert.

This is the goal of meditation, to become still and watch our thoughts, to recognize the thoughts, beliefs, and assumptions we hold deep down. To become aware of our thought patterns. To disidentify from our thoughts and not take each thought too seriously.

The goal is to become conscious creators of our reality. Only from a place of stillness are we able to produce conscious thoughts. Only from a place of awareness are we able to create our reality with intention.

Magic

Life is magic, and we are the magicians. In every moment, we are performing the art of creation, turning our thoughts into reality, turning intention into action. Sending messages to the universe and receiving guidance from beyond. In each moment we are both witnessing and participating in the miracle of life.

Life is the dance and we are the dancer. We bring Source energy into manifestation, into our reality. By making our wishes come true, we make magic. We are powerful creatures sent to the earth to discover its secrets. To witness its beauty. To realize its magnificence.

We have infinite creative potential hidden deep within us, if we only dare to look. With our kindness, we uplift others and perform the magic of love. With our kind deeds, we bring out the goodness within us. We bring the magic into our reality. We are magicians, always in the process of creation.

Infinite

We are infinite like the universe. Our heart is as deep as the ocean. We are limitless creatures with infinite potential hidden inside us; with potential to create. Potential to grow. We bring with us divine energy from the world beyond. From the Unmanifest. We hold within us all the wonders of the world.

Deep within our souls, we have an urge to create; a desire to manifest our dreams. A longing to show who we really are. We are Source made manifest. We are one with the divine. What we can accomplish is beyond our imagination. Who we have the potential to be is beyond description. Our soul is as vast as the sky. We are infinite, creative beings.

Intuition

Intuition is our soul guiding us. It is our heart speaking to us, telling us which direction to take. Intuition is a deep knowing. A clairvoyance. An intelligence that is not of this world; an intelligence that cannot be explained with logic. It's a lamp that guides us; a light that shows us the way.

Intuition is a strong pull towards what is right; a gravitation towards truth. Intuition is our gut feeling, a message that comes from deep within us. It is the supreme form of knowing—a knowing that is beyond the mind. It is ultimate wisdom. It is guidance from our inner being. We must learn to pay attention to the messages we receive from our soul. We have to learn to trust our gut feeling. Our intuition will guide us in our darkest times. We must trust and obey our most powerful source of guidance. We must trust our intuition.

World of Form

Look at the world of form and recognize its fleeting nature. Notice how forms arise and how they dissipate. Notice how circumstances come and go; how life forms go through the cycle of birth and death. Notice the ephemeral nature of everything in this world. It is in the nature of things to change. It is natural for forms to arise and dissolve.

Recognize the inherent instability in everything around you. Every form, every circumstance, and every living being is constantly changing. The world is always evolving. Don't seek stability in the world of form, the physical world, the dimension of time and space. Don't attach yourself to any place, person, or object, nor to any circumstance or mental identity. The world of form is fleeting. Recognize this and see the beauty in it. Find the magnificence inherent in this ever-changing world. Become a river and flow with the changes of life. Embrace it.

The Ego

The ego is the phantom self—a false sense of self. It is a mind-made entity of who we are. It is an illusion. When we react to things, when we take things personally, our ego is active. When we feel we are victims or have a grandiose image of ourselves, that's the ego. When we feel a sense of separateness, that's ego.

The ego shouldn't be taken too seriously. It is not who we really are. It is only a shadow. A false image. The ego is here for a purpose. It is here to guide us; to show us our shadow self. To show us what we need to work on. Where we need healing. We have to recognize the ego for what it is. We must learn to become aware of it when it arises. We should never mistakenly identify with it. We only have to observe and learn from it. We only have to see where it's pointing to. Through the ego, we learn where our trigger points are. We learn where there is unhealed trauma. That is the purpose of the ego. But it is not who we are. We are pure spirits.

Pure Bliss

In the depth of our soul, we are pure bliss. In our innermost being, we are pure joy. Our deeper self, our spirit, is unshakeable. It exists beyond time and space. It resides in a place beyond duality, beyond the seemingly opposing forces. Deep in the core of our being, we are made whole and complete. We are made perfect in the mirror image of the Creator. We are divinity expressed in human form. Our holy essence shines through our seemingly solid form. We come from the Unmanifest, looking for a way to express. At the centre of our being, there is nothing that we lack. The entire universe exists within every cell of our body. We are one with Source. We are divine.

Synchronicity

Have you ever felt things falling into place on their own? Have you ever had questions in your mind that were answered spontaneously? Have you ever felt like there are just too many coincidences and there must be a larger force at play? This is synchronicity, a wink from the universe, letting us know it has our back. Showing us that it's working things out in our favor. Reminding us that it is our guide, helping us through challenges, guiding us in reaching our purpose. Communicating with us through everything around us. Reminding us of our divine nature.

Synchronicity happens when we are aligned, when we are grounded. When we have a deep trust in the universe. When we feel connected. Synchronicity is like a rhythm. A harmony. A spark from the universe, leading us towards our purpose. It is pure magic.

Brilliant

Dare to be different. Dare to be brilliant. Dare to make your dreams come true. Forget about doubt and fear. Only believe. Know in your heart that you can achieve whatever you put your mind and heart into. Know that at your core you are a brilliant, magnificent being of light. Know that you were born to be joyful. You were meant to live an abundant life. Know that nothing can hold you back. Nothing can come in between you and your dreams. Recognize the depth of your own being. The depth of your own soul. Recognize your brilliance. You are limitless.

Soul Purpose

Our sole purpose—our *soul* purpose—is to love and be loved.

Our sole purpose is to bring light into this world, to recognize the depth of our own soul, the vastness of who we are.

Our soul purpose is to remember who we really are; to remember that we are infinite beings of light; that we are pure spirit manifesting in human form. Our soul purpose is to recognize our own being, to see the light within our hearts. To send love out into the universe. To show who we really are. To allow our inner nature to emerge.

This is our sole purpose. It is our *soul* purpose.

Stardust

We come from beyond the galaxies, from beyond this realm. We come from another dimension. We are soul manifesting a body. Our spirit is ethereal. Our spirit is pure light. Our body is a portal containing divine energy; it contains our true selves. What we are is infinite life and pure bliss. We are one with the sky, the earth, the sun, and the moon. We exist within every drop in every ocean. We appear in every star in the cosmos. We are galactic beings of light, bringing with us infinite love and joy. We manifest the divine beauty, the divine essence. We are pure stardust.

Joy of Being

Sometimes we get so caught up in the things we're doing, we forget about the joy of being. Sometimes we get so entangled with our everyday activities, we forget to take time for ourselves. We forget to pause and reflect. We forget to incorporate stillness into our lives. We forget the essence of our soul and the deep joy that resides within us.

Sometimes we fall prey to the belief that we must achieve this or that to feel happy. Sometimes we run on autopilot. Sometimes we focus so much on our goal that we miss the moment. We miss the gift of the here and now. It is so important to recognize when this happens and take a break. It is so vital to take time and go inward. We have to take time to fully be with ourselves and enjoy our own being, our own presence. Even though many things we do in life bring us joy and happiness, they cannot replace the joy of *being*. The joy of being is the ultimate form of happiness. The ultimate joy. To be fully present with ourselves and enjoy our own company—that is the real secret.

Travelers

We are travelers that come from beyond. We are travelers who come from the galaxies, walking on this planet we call earth. We are here to discover the secrets of the universe. We are here to understand ourselves. With this inner knowledge, we come to know our own abilities, our own brilliance. With this understanding, we start to make great discoveries. We come to know that we are one with the universe; that nothing is outside of us. That everything we are looking for, we hold within. That everything we seek is already inside us.

As we come to realize the infinite nature of the universe, we realize that we too are infinite. We realize that we are limitless and that nothing can define us. Nothing can contain us. We realize the vast powers we hold. We realize that we are intergalactic beings and earth is our temporary home. The more we recognize our infinite nature, the more we believe in our own abilities. We realize that we can accomplish anything. We are travelers from beyond.

Anger

Anger is a strange emotion. It is explosive energy that starts from the solar plexus and makes its way up. We have a narrow window to become aware of it before it comes to the foreground. Otherwise, we will sink into a lower level of consciousness and lose awareness of what we are doing or saying. It's as if the anger is a person of its own. It is its own entity. Which is why when we come out of a state of anger, we often say, "I don't know what came over me."

The anger is not who we are. It is only trapped energy that has built up from negativity. Anger is a tricky emotion. It is more difficult to bring into the level of awareness. But look closer, and you will find that behind anger, there is fear. Look even closer and you will find that behind fear, there is grief.

We have to strip away all the layers to see anger for what it is, to recognize where it comes from. We have to look at our own pain to be able to control our anger, instead of letting it control us. We have to honestly look within ourselves and see where the fear is coming from. Otherwise, we will become victims of our own anger over and over again. By looking deeply into our own pain and our own fear, we gain the ability to dissolve negativity, to dissolve anger. By raising our level of awareness, we can become aware of our own anger whenever it arises in us. We are not anger—or any emotion we experience. Anything that comes and goes is not us. We are the observer underneath. We are stillness.

Artist

You are an artist, and life is your canvas. You can paint it all the colors you like. You can create whatever you want out of it. You can bring into existence whatever it is your heart desires. Your work of art is a continuous project. Your masterpiece is a lifelong journey. You are always in the process of creation. You are creating your life in every moment. You are deciding in each moment who you want to be. So pick up your paintbrush and paint your canvas all the colors of your heart. Close your eyes. Imagine what it is you want to create and bring it onto your canvas. Turn that into your artwork. Look at your painting. Reflect. See if it is complete. See if it represents your soul. Where it doesn't resonate, grab your paintbrush and change the colors. Adjust your painting. Life is your canvas, and you are always painting it. You are always creating art from it. Allow yourself the freedom to paint what you want from your heart. You are an artist.

Journey of the Soul

The journey of the soul is not a clear path. It is filled with obstacles and challenges. Many lessons are concealed within every situation that the soul must learn. There are many barriers the soul must overcome. The journey of the soul, the path to self-realization, is a lifelong journey. On this journey, what matters is not where we stand or what we achieve. What matters is how we are being. Our presence, our internal state, is what truly matters. Are we coming from a place of love? Are we being true to ourselves? Are we doing things that bring us joy? These are the questions that truly matter. These are the things we must consider on our journey. The soul is always seeking light. Always seeking truth. We must always stay present and aware on the journey of our soul.

                                   SARA BIGHASH

Cure

Don't lose yourself in your pain. Know that for every pain, there is a cure. Know that after every hardship, there is ease. Know that every pain will dissolve. Healing energy is always available to us. The light within us heals us. The kindness, love, and peace in our own heart is our remedy.

We must not stay long in despair. There is always hope. There is always light, even in our darkest days. Sadness and grief are only temporary feelings that fade away. By using the light of our presence, we can dissolve past pain. We can heal ourselves. We do not need to carry sadness with us. It will go of its own accord. There is always a remedy for every ailment. There is a cure. There is healing for every pain. There is always hope lying amidst despair.

Key to Life

The key to life is to want what you have. It is to fully accept what is. The key to life is to be in alignment with the here and now, to offer no resistance to the present moment. To offer no resistance to life. We often construct a mental image of what our life should look like, an image of where we're supposed to be. But rarely does our reality line up exactly with our mental image. There are always imperfections. There are always challenges. There are always things we may not have imagined. The secret is to pretend like we have chosen everything in our life. By adopting this mentality, we no longer see ourselves as victims of circumstances. We no longer feel powerless. By completely accepting what is and pretending as though we have chosen it, we feel we have power to act. We feel we have power to create change; to either change the situation, or change our mindset about it, to shift how we see things. This way, we are realigned with life and we reclaim our power. This way, *we* are the ones exerting influence instead of being influenced by external factors.

Always want what you have in life. Watch how it changes everything. Watch how it will make miracles happen.

Catch Yourself

Whenever you find yourself falling into negative thinking, catch yourself. Whenever you find your mind wandering and telling you stories of the past, become aware. Break the cycle. Break the thought pattern. Create a gap in your thinking. Instead of identifying with your thoughts, step back and observe them. Instead of identifying with your mind, observe your mind. Become the witnessing presence. Allow the thoughts to rise up and disappear, like watching the clouds in the sky. Nothing about them is personal. They are only thoughts. They are only mental formations. Don't take each thought seriously.

Whenever you find yourself judging yourself or other people, step out of your mind. Whenever you find yourself complaining about what is or what should be, detach yourself from thinking and observe. By becoming aware of our thoughts, we regain the power of our presence. We regain the power to act according to what the situation needs. We see things clearly again, as they are, not through a lens of the past. Not through the lens of the conditioned mind. We are not our mind. We are the stillness underneath it. We are pure consciousness. Pure awareness.

Let Go

Learn to let go of everything that no longer serves you. If there is grief from your past, acknowledge it, allow it space to be, feel it fully, then let it go. If there is a person you miss but is no longer in your life, acknowledge the feeling, remember them, send them love, and then let them go. If you have lost something of value, acknowledge the feeling, honor the feeling, and let it go. If you feel anger towards someone for something they may have done, recognize the feeling, allow it space to be, wish that person love and healing, and let them go.

Know that letting go of unnecessary mental baggage is one of the most powerful things you can do. Know that living lightly is living freely. Know that a life free of guilt, blame, grudges, or any form of negativity, is pure joy. We must learn to continuously let go of things, not allow them to build up inside of us. We must not allow anything to dim our light. Not allow the ebbs and flows of life or the pains we experience to go inside us. We must learn to always maintain our peace, to always come home to ourselves. To always live in presence, in joy. Learn to let go of everything that doesn't serve you. Let go of everything that makes you feel heavy. You were meant to live a free and joyful life.

Challenge Yourself

Challenge yourself to see the good in every situation, to see the wisdom hidden within anything that falls apart. See the lessons concealed within every failure or defeat. See beyond the world of duality, beyond the apparent good and bad, and recognize that every situation is neutral from a higher perspective. Challenge yourself to see obstacles as opportunities for growth. Ask yourself, what is in this situation? What can I learn? Challenge yourself to see that something you have lost may have saved you from pain, to see that things falling apart create space for something new to arise in your life. For new energy to come in. Challenge yourself to question your own beliefs on what is good or bad or what you think your life should look like. Challenge yourself to recognize all the things you have that you once prayed for, before complaining about lack. Challenge yourself to see the full cup in every circumstance, no matter how difficult it may appear. There is good hidden within every situation. Blessings are concealed within every difficulty. The key is to find them.

Meaning

Each event is neutral from a higher perspective. Each circumstance or situation doesn't by itself shape us or create who we are. It's the meaning we give them that makes us who we are. It's how we make sense of it that shapes who we become. Meaning is everything. The meaning we assign to a situation or event determines how we see it. It determines how we allow it to shape us. It determines what we will gain from it and how we are going to use it.

Whether we see an event as a barrier or as a guide in helping us grow is up to us. Whether we see a past event as having defeated us or having made us stronger is up to us. Life is always happening. Circumstances are always changing, and we are always presented with challenges in one form or another. We may experience challenges different from one another, and some of us may experience challenges that are far more difficult than others. But the meaning we assign them is up to us. We have the power to determine how a situation is going to define us and shape who we become. We have the power to assign meaning.

SARA BIGHASH

Facing our Fears

Every time we face our fears, we gain strength and courage. Each time we do what scares us, we start to believe in our own power. We start to believe in ourselves and slowly, doubt fades away and bravery takes its place. We have untapped potential within us that, if only we knew, would make our fears look so small in comparison. By facing our fears, we tap into our potential. We awaken the dormant energy that lies within us. We awaken our spirit. The more we do things that scare us, the more we nurture our inner powers and the more we grow. The more we step out of our comfort zone, the more fearless we become. Whether it is fear of failure, or loss, or criticism, by pursuing what we want despite the fear, we go beyond it. By doing this, we live from the heart. We operate from a place of love. Sometimes, we may even be afraid of the unknown when we want to create change or start something new. But there is so much beauty in the unknown. So much wisdom in uncertainty. If we were sure of everything in our lives, if our life was planned for us, there would be no deeper meaning to anything. There would be no mystery, no element of play.

Life consists of gifts that we must dare to unwrap. Every step of the journey is a present. Dare to conquer your fears and rise above them. Dare to push your own boundaries.

Today is a Gift

Today is a gift. That's why they call it the present. The Buddha said, "Every morning we are born again. What we do today is what matters most." Indeed, every day is a gift. Every day we get to wake up and start over. Each day is a rebirth. Each day is a blessing. If we truly recognize this truth, our perception of life will change. If we truly understand that each day we are gifted with a fresh start, we will act more graciously. We will act out of love. If we understand that we must only conquer the day and not our entire life, we will go deeper in the heart. We will start acting on our priorities and dedicating time and energy to the things that truly matter to us. We will become more present and truly appreciate the here and now, rather than projecting ourselves into the future. We come to realize that each new day is ours and we get to decide what we do with it. We decide what our state of mind will be. We decide what we will do and how we are going to do it. We take power back. Each day, we have the opportunity to do what brings us joy and happiness. Each day is a chance for us to express what is in our heart. Each day we have the opportunity to say unspoken words and to express our love and gratitude for the people close to us. Each day is a chance to allow new energy in and old energy out. You don't have to figure out your entire life. Just conquer the day, and you have already conquered your life.

As Within, So Without

We will see in the world what we hold in our heart. Whatever we believe deep down, we will see around us. Whatever is in our heart and mind will be reflected in one way or another in the outside world. As the mystic saying goes, "As within, so without." If we believe in goodness, we will see it reflected in people and circumstances. If we believe in love, we will see loving-kindness all around us. Similarly, if we believe in malicious intentions, we will see it reflected in the world.

Life is a mirror, and we see ourselves reflected in it. If we believe that the world is ultimately good and the universe has our back, we will persevere and have faith in our heart, even in the most difficult circumstances. But if we believe that the world is a scary place and we are separate from the universe, we will be disheartened with the slightest challenge.

We have to deeply examine our own heart. We have to take care of our inner world. Because we will see it reflected in our reality.

Higher Self

Our higher self is always with us, guiding us on our life journey. It is our higher consciousness. It is always telling us the right thing to do. It's always guiding us from beyond. It's the inner feeling that tells us what course of action to take in difficult times. It's an inner knowing that tells us when we're doing something that is out of alignment. It is always nudging us in the right direction. Sometimes when we are in a difficult situation and don't know what to do, we have to ask our higher self. When something no longer serves us and we need to create change, we must look to our higher self. Our higher self always guides us towards light, towards love. It is always leading us to the truth of our own soul.

Sometimes we are afraid of losing something, but our higher self tells us to let it go. And we know that it's for a greater purpose. It's for our soul's growth. Sometimes when we're going through pain and suffering, our higher self reminds us that everything is temporary. It guides us to a deep sense of peace. It guides us towards serenity. It reminds us of what is truly important in life. It helps us see the bigger picture. Our higher self is the wisdom that we hold. An inner knowing. It is our Spirit guide.

     SARA BIGHASH

Vibrations

We cannot force a connection. We meet the right people at the right time through natural vibration. We connect with others through energy. Our soul is always reading people's energy and giving us signs. We often get a vibe from someone even before words are exchanged.

There is an energetic field where communication is always taking place. That field is always operating, and we are always reading energy. What we feel in our heart and our gut is much stronger than the mind. Sometimes we have a negative gut reaction towards someone. It is our soul rejecting them. It means our energies do not match. Sometimes we feel drawn towards someone and our heart feels peace when we speak with them. We feel a natural gravitation towards that person. There's a coherency between our energies. Vibes are much stronger than thoughts. If we listen, our inner body is always telling us how it feels through vibration, through gut reaction. We just have to pay attention.

Value Yourself

Always value yourself. Recognize your own divinity. Recognize the power of your own being. Know that your time and energy are valuable. When you give your time and energy to a person or a task, you are sharing your presence. Know that your presence is the most valuable gift you have. Know that your presence is the most precious thing you can give someone or dedicate to something. So be careful who you share your presence with. Make sure to surround yourself with those that value you. Make sure to share your spirit with those who wish to see your growth. Those who want to see you excel. Those who want to see you happy and joyful. Make sure that whatever task you dedicate your time and energy to is worthwhile. Make sure it is what you truly want to do. Make sure it is something you enjoy, and not just a means to an end. If you are doing something simply because you have to, bring loving energy into it. Dedicate your presence to it. Because when you value yourself, you realize that no matter what you are doing, you deserve to be happy. You can choose to be joyful. Value yourself, and know that the gift of your presence is the greatest gift you have.

Purify your Heart

We must clear our hearts of any form of impurity. We must clear our hearts of any malice or ill intention. We must rid ourselves of any judgement, jealousy, envy, hate, grudge, or despair. We must learn to completely love and accept ourselves. When we feel peace within ourselves, we also feel at peace with others. When we hold love and compassion for ourselves, we naturally feel love and compassion for other people. We no longer feel the need to judge or criticize, to find fault or to envy. We no longer feel the need to compare ourselves to anybody. We do not feel like we are above or beneath anyone.

By purifying our hearts, we realize we are equal to all. The hate, jealousy, or envy in our heart dissipates as love, which is an infinitely more powerful force, takes its place. As we cleanse our hearts, we come to great spiritual realizations. We see the world more clearly. We find that the essence of the universe is love. We feel lighter. We feel the force of love within our inner being. We feel its vital energy expanding our soul. As we purify our hearts, we live deeper in the spirit.

Clarity

Sometimes, in the midst of chaos, we find clarity. Sometimes, in our darkest times, we find our own light. We find our power. In our pain, we find our strength. Just as gold is refined by fire, we grow through our hardships. Just as diamonds are formed under intense pressure, we are transformed into stronger versions of ourselves by withstanding difficulties and challenges.

Hard times, although they may not appear so while we're experiencing them, are what shape us. They reveal to us our hidden power. They force us to use inner strength we didn't know we had. They force us to tap into our hidden potential, a reservoir of energy and abilities we have stored within us. Difficulties and challenges take us from our elementary states and turn us into refined versions of ourselves. They turn us into warriors. They force us to use wisdom and inner knowledge we were unaware of. They take us to a place of deep realization. They take us into spiritual depth.

It is during difficult times that we realize how powerful we are. It is during these times that we become fearless and start believing in ourselves. It is during these times that we get to re-examine our beliefs and values. We get to redefine our life purpose and reorganize our priorities. We start living from our spirit rather than the mind. During these times, we discover our own depth.

This Too Shall Pass

Whenever you are dealing with difficult circumstances or you find yourself in a negative state, just know that everything is temporary. Whenever you feel like you've lost hope, know that *This too shall pass.* It is in the nature of things to change. Circumstances arise and dissolve. Various challenges come and go. Life has its ebbs and flows. Don't hold onto anything. Let everything go. Don't let sadness, fear, anxiety, or anger stay with you long. Learn to let them go as they arise. Don't let any form of negativity build up inside you. Allow the light of your consciousness to dissolve whatever negativity arises. Allow your presence to dissolve pain from the past.

By living completely in the now, you start to let go of unnecessary baggage. You allow space for any sadness or frustration that may arise to subside. By giving them space, you allow them to be released from your aura. Whenever a negative emotion arises within you, become completely present. Radiate the light of your consciousness on the feeling so it may subside. Never hold onto negative feelings. Allow them space and let them go. Don't go into despair. Know that every situation will change.

     SARA BIGHASH

Beauty in Loss

Sometimes we grieve over what we have lost. Sometimes we think we have lost part of ourselves or something of great value. But if we look deeper, we find that often, the losses we experience happen for a higher purpose. We find that the universe is creating space so something better can come into our lives. It is dissolving old energy and making room for new energy to enter. Loss is a natural part of life. Without it, we would only be accumulating, and there would be no space for anything new to arise. We lose cells in our body every day as new cells are created. We are losing parts of our old self every day as our new self emerges. There is beauty in loss. We must acknowledge and honor it.

Essence

Do you know who you really are? You are beyond anything you can fathom. Your true essence is pure love, pure light. You are the universe expressing itself in human form. Your true essence comes from beyond. It comes from another realm. You are not the form you appear in. You cannot be defined by any conceptual identity. The essence of who you are cannot be found in a name or a title. It cannot be found in this world. Even though you appear in earthly form, you are not from the earth. You come from beyond the stars. You are pure spirit. Pure divinity. Recognize your true essence and return to the root of your own soul. You are divine.

The Mind

The mind is a powerful tool. Everything we create is first created in our minds. We create our reality with our mind through our deep-seated beliefs and thoughts. Thoughts are energy. Each thought has a vibrational frequency. Thoughts turn into words and then action. Words amplify the energy of thoughts. Actions accelerate the energy behind thoughts. We manifest through thoughts, words, and actions.

But we have to be careful how we create. Are we creating consciously or unconsciously? Are we aware of our own thoughts or are we letting them roam free? When we create unconsciously, we create more of the past. When we create consciously, we create what we desire. We create by choice. By creating a gap between us and our thoughts, by becoming the observer, we become conscious of our thoughts. We get to manifest with awareness. The mind is powerful, but we have to use it wisely.

Rise Above

Sometimes we are presented with challenges that seem beyond our capacity to handle. Sometimes when we are going through hardship, we can't see the other side. During these times, we have to remember that we can always rise above. No matter how difficult the situation may seem, we can always come out the other side stronger. If we open our heart and if we allow it, we can let the situation make us more humble, more compassionate. If we let it, the difficulties can make us more human. So no matter what obstacles or challenges you are faced with, know that you can rise above.

SARA BIGHASH

Compassion

Imagine if each time we met someone, their entire life would flash before our eyes. We would witness everything they have been through. All their joy. All their pain. We'd be in their shoes for their entire life journey in a split second. All their moments of happiness and their moments of anguish. All the difficulties they have been through. This would dramatically change how we relate to other people. We would immediately feel love and compassion for them. We would come from a place of deep understanding rather than a place of judgement. We would see ourselves as one with the other person.

We would realize that ultimately, we have felt the same emotions. We would recognize their pain as our pain and their joy as our joy. The boundaries of ego would dissolve, and we would feel connected on the level of being. We would feel a deep, empathetic resonance with others. We would no longer find any reason to judge or criticize one another.

If we cultivate deep understanding and compassion within ourselves, we will be able to better relate to others. Love will naturally arise in our interactions and our relationships as we come out of the illusion of separation.

Nature

Go outside into nature and feel its healing energy. Allow its vibrancy to soothe your soul. Allow it to ground you. Feel from deep within the connection between you and nature—the connection between you and everything else. Allow nature to bring you back into stillness, into the present moment. Allow it to shift your awareness to the here and now. Feel the essence of your own being as you connect with nature. Recognize its essence as one with your own. Look at the beauty in everything around you and find yourself reflected in it.

Let nature teach you the law of patience. Let it teach you how it does not hurry, yet everything is accomplished. Let it show you how every tree, every plant, every flower flows with the rhythm of life. Let it show you how the energy force within you is the same energy force within every other being. Let yourself be awestruck and inspired by nature, by its inherent harmony—by its ineffability. See the interconnectedness of everything around you and recognize the divinity within everything. Realize you are divine. Let nature take you back to your own roots.

Beauty of the Butterfly

The butterfly is such a beautiful and elegant creature. It is so captivating and mesmerizing. When you see a butterfly, you can sense its ethereal nature, you can feel its vibrancy. The butterfly is very unique. It teaches us many secrets through its way of life. The butterfly lives freely and lightly. It drinks the nectar of one flower and then flies off to the next. It is always seeking new adventures.

The butterfly teaches us not to settle. It teaches us to always seek new experiences and always grow. It shows us to live free and not attach ourselves to anything. The butterfly is tricky. If you try to catch it, it will only fly away from you. But if you are still and only observe, it just might fly in your direction.

The butterfly teaches us that if we develop stillness within ourselves, the things we want will come to us. It teaches us that we don't need to chase happiness. If we remain in inner stillness, in inner peace, happiness and joy will naturally arise within us. The butterfly teaches us to live freely and to enjoy the pure bliss of life.

Skyscraper

Take the stones along your path and build a skyscraper. Take the obstacles in your path and turn them into your assets. Perform alchemy and turn your deepest pains into your greatest strengths. Take your triggers and make them your guru. Let them show you the path. Let them take you to your higher self. Let them make you wiser. Don't allow yourself to trip over the stones in your path. Instead, pick them up and make them your tools. Become a builder. The skyscraper you build is evidence of the hardship you've endured. It is evidence of your resilience in the face of adversity. Know that whatever obstacle you are faced with in life, it is your quest to overcome. Take each barrier, each lesson, and let it shape you into the person you strive to be. Let it make you stronger.

Power of Writing

There is so much power in writing. Through writing, we can express ourselves. We can organize our thoughts. We can cleanse our minds. We can put our heart and soul on paper. We can share with others what is deep inside us. We can share ideas with people both near and far. Someone somewhere else could be reading what you wrote and know exactly how you feel. They can feel the words come to life. They can feel the energy behind the words. Through writing, we can break barriers and create bridges. We can build connections with people we've never met. We can build an empathetic resonance with people we don't know. We can make someone feel understood. We can deepen our relationships with those in our lives. Writing has the power to take us into another person's heart and soul. The power of writing is ineffable.

There is No Separation

Those we love, we love from heart. Those we hold dear are close to our spirit. Distance does not separate people. In true friendship, in true love, there is no separation. Our love and caring for someone extends beyond land and ocean. Our love goes beyond any physical distance in the world. Our love goes into the heart and spirit of whomever we love. Our love is a vibrational frequency in our heart. It's a bond between us and the other. When we love someone, we hold them in our thoughts. We hold space for them in our hearts and send them love and good intentions. Love always connects us. True friendship always endures.

True Friend

A true friend is one who uplifts you when you're feeling down. A true friend is someone who wants to see you excel, one who wants to see you succeed. A true friend is one who supports your growth, one who helps you reach your higher self. One who encourages you to break your boundaries and face your fears. A true friend is someone who stands beside you during your darkest times, one who creates space for you and listens to you. One who allows you to be unapologetically yourself. One who makes you feel free.

A true friend is someone who understands you, someone who withholds judgement and holds you in their loving embrace. A true friend is one who tells you the truth, even when it may be hard to hear. Even when it may be unpleasant. A true friend is always honest with you and helps you push through difficulty. A true friend is one who acknowledges and appreciates your good qualities but also points out your weakness and where you need to work, when necessary.

A true friend is one who reflects back to you the love and kindness you hold within your heart. A true friend is a gift. A guide to your higher purpose in life. A true friend is always with you in heart and spirit.

Self-Sufficient

You are holy. You are whole. You were made in the mirror image of the divine. You reflect divinity. You were made perfect, reflecting the perfection of the Creator. At the core of your being, there is nothing you lack. You were made whole and complete. Everything you want in this world is already within you. You simply have to direct your attention within and recognize the depth of your own soul. Recognize the beauty that lies at the core of your being. Realize that you are a creature of light. By recognizing the light within you, you bring light into this world. By recognizing the magnificence of your own being, you bring your magnificence into this world. Recognize the power of your own being. Recognize your divine essence. You are always whole. Always complete.

Open Your Mind

When we open our mind, we break out of old thinking patterns. We let go of preconceived ideas and assumptions. We break boundaries and limitations. We break down the walls of ego. When we open our mind, we open our heart and soul to the realm of infinite possibilities. We open ourselves to the vastness of the universe. We allow new knowledge, new ways of knowing, to flow to us. We allow new energy to come into our lives.

By opening our mind, we learn to grow and evolve. We learn to flow with life and not attach ourselves to any mental concepts or notions. We learn to live more freely. We learn to live in spirit. By opening our mind, we open ourselves to the universe. We open ourselves to infinity.

Growth

Growth is not just about attaining things. Growth is just as much about letting go as it is about achievement. It's about letting go of what does not serve us. It's about letting go of old thinking patterns that were keeping us in the past. It's about letting go of limiting beliefs.

Growth is when we let go of fear and doubt and live from a place of love and trust. It's when we start living in our hearts rather than in our minds. Growth is when we no longer identify with our past. It's when we no longer see ourselves through past pain or a conceptual identity. It's when we let go of unnecessary baggage and allow new energy to enter our lives. It's when we let go of who we *think* we are, so that who we *really* are can emerge.

Growth means no longer reacting to things, but finding a way to properly respond to them. Growth means healing pain from the past and using the wisdom we gained from it. It means coming from a place of love rather than defense. Growth is when we step out of our comfort zone and recognize our true power. It's when we realize our souls are infinite and unshakeable. It's when we become aware of the impact of our words and actions and use them to spread positivity.

Growth is when we see beyond ourselves and recognize our oneness with everyone. Growth is when we extend ourselves and uplift others.

Count Your Blessings

So often, we ask for things in prayer but forget to acknowledge all the blessings we already have. We forget that what we have today is what we prayed for yesterday. We forget that we have blessings today that in the past, we wouldn't have even imagined. We sometimes forget about all of our wishes that have come true. All of the miracles that have happened in our lives. All of the times we were showered with love by the universe in unexpected ways.

We forget about unanswered prayers that turned out to be in our favor. We forget about how many times we were saved by grace from disaster. So, before we pray for new things to manifest in our lives, before we ask the universe for more favors, we have to acknowledge and appreciate what we already have. We have to count our blessings.

Make it a practice to become aware of all the blessings in your life and give thanks for them in prayer before asking for anything new. Envision your blessings and feel gratitude fill your heart. Acknowledging the good already in our lives is the foundation for all abundance.

Compass

Our soul is our compass, always guiding us in the right direction, always leading us on our life journey. The soul always knows what it wants. It always knows the right thing to do. All we have to do is listen to it. All we have to do is pay attention to the inner voice, the inner knowing. We have to pay attention to what we are naturally drawn to. Those are the things that resonate with our soul. Those are the things that bring us deep joy.

When we are in doubt or stumble upon a fork in the road, we have to ask our soul for guidance. It always knows the way. Sometimes it is difficult to hear what our soul is trying to tell us because of the noise in our mind. We have to learn how to quiet our mind and listen to our soul. We have to trust the inner guidance.

Sometimes it is not apparent at first what our soul is trying to tell us. We have to learn to decodify its language and uncover the hidden messages it is giving us. Sometimes it is not clear where our soul is guiding us. We just have to trust. We just have to follow one step at a time and have faith. The soul is our compass. It is always guiding us toward our purpose.

Inner Bond

We often think that we connect with people through words. We may think that our friendships have formed through conversation. Yet words only serve as a pretext. They are only tools that we use to communicate. On a deeper level, it is an inner bond that draws us to people. We connect with others on an energetic level. We form friendships through a resonance in the heart. It is a natural gravitation that draws us towards certain people. It is an inner knowing. Although we may share thoughts and ideas through words, we connect on the level of being. We connect through the vibration of the heart. Love and friendships are formed through an inner bond.

Blessing in Disguise

Often in life, we don't understand why certain things happen or why they happen the way they do. Many times, we find ourselves in a situation that at first may seem dreadful. Yet that situation could be, and often is, a blessing in disguise. Often what appears to us as a negative situation turns out to be in our favor. Sometimes it is through seemingly adverse circumstances that doors begin to open for us. We never really know the true nature of a situation. We tend to make judgements based on our own perception of good and bad. We categorize and label circumstances based on our own limited perceptions.

Sometimes it is in our darkest times that we come to great realizations. Sometimes when things fall apart, it creates space for new things to emerge. Often, through seemingly adverse circumstances, life forces us to make changes that we would be hesitant to make otherwise. Sometimes life pushes us out of our comfort zone so we can grow. In every seemingly negative situation, there lies great opportunity. The key is to find it.

The Path

We often think that the path is our goal, our destination. We think obstacles block us along our path. What we don't realize is that obstacles *are* the path. The barriers are what we must learn to overcome. The boundaries we face are our quest. Each time we overcome an obstacle, we gain courage. We learn new lessons and become wiser. Each time we push through a barrier, we break our own limitations and expand ourselves. Each time we overcome adversity, we become stronger.

It is not getting to the final destination that makes us who we are. It is all the challenges we face and all the difficulties we overcome along our path that shape us. They are what build our character. Our journey is not an end goal. Our journey is growth.

Transformation

The greatest gift you can give the world is that of your own transformation. When you transform yourself, when you grow, you gain the strength and the ability to help others grow. By lifting yourself up, you are able to lift those around you and show them their own strength. It is only when we improve ourselves that we can help others improve. It is when we find our own path that we can help others find theirs.

Everything starts with us. We have to transform ourselves first to be able to add value to others. By enriching our own spirit and our own lives, we can help enrich others' lives. We must have in order to give. One cannot pour from an empty cup. We must fill our own cup so we can share with others.

Metamorphosis

There comes a time on our spiritual journey when we find that we are no longer the person we used to be. We no longer recognize our old self. We know something has changed. Yet at the same time, our new self hasn't fully emerged yet. It is still forming.

It is during this middle stage in growth that we may feel lost—just like the metamorphosis of a butterfly when it is in a cocoon; no longer a caterpillar and not yet a butterfly. During this stage, we may feel confused. We may feel empty. But this is just a phase. It is part of the journey of transformation. It is when we've let go of the old but the new hasn't fully emerged yet.

We may feel like we are in an empty space. We may feel like we are in a no-man's-land. We simply have to be patient and trust the process. We have to trust with our heart that everything will fall into place in its own time.

Resilience

One of the most amazing things in life is the resilience of the human spirit. It is amazing how some people go through extreme pain and agony in their life and come out the other side stronger. It is amazing how the human spirit can endure so much hardship and heal. The human spirit is unshakeable. It has such enormous strength. It has the ability to turn the deepest pains into its greatest assets. It can perform alchemy and turn darkness into light.

Some of the most kind and gentle people on the planet are those who've endured extreme suffering. Some of the most loving and healing souls are the ones who've gone through extreme hardship in their lives. Many people who've had difficult lives have made it their mission to reduce human suffering as much as possible. It is evident that despite circumstances and conditioning, the human spirit is innately drawn to the light. It holds the light within and wants to share it.

Spread Positivity

Wherever you are and whatever you are doing, make it your intention to spread love and kindness. Make it your mission to spread positivity. With kind words, a smile, a nice gesture, you can start a ripple effect. You can become a force that spreads love and light. You can uplift those around you. You can nourish the seeds of positivity within others. You can be an agent for positive change.

With your thoughts, words, and actions, you can change the world for yourself and those around you. You can even impact those you've never met through the domino effect of kindness. Hold the light that is within your heart and choose to share it with others wherever you are. Never underestimate your own powers.

 SARA BIGHASH

Higher Vibrations

Move out of the tangle of fear-based thinking and come towards love. Free yourself from fear and doubt and recognize your own abilities. Start believing in yourself. Believe that you can achieve whatever you set out to do; whatever you pursue with heart and spirit. Raise your vibration by living from a place of love and trust by knowing your own value, by recognizing your divine nature. By doing things from your soul.

Recognize that life itself is a miracle and you are the source of joy. You are pure bliss. Start noticing the good all around you and live in gratitude. Raise your vibration by spreading the light and love that is within your heart.

Night Sky

Have you ever looked at the night sky and felt mesmerized by its beauty? Have you ever been captivated by the vastness of space? Have you ever wondered how many stars and galaxies there are out there?

Space is vast indeed. Ultimately, the universe is made up of mostly empty space. When we feel awestruck by space, we recognize it as the same space within us. Our soul is vast like the universe. The depth we perceive out there in the beautiful night sky is also within us. We are a microcosm of the universe. We hold within us all the stars and the galaxies. We have unimaginable depth and beauty within us.

Let the vastness of the sky take you deep into stillness and recognize the depth of your own being.

Meditate

Go deep into your meditation with intention. Observe your thoughts like clouds in the sky. Watch your thoughts come and go. Watch as each thought arises and then subsides. Observe the space between you and your thoughts. Feel your inner being as you observe. Go deeper into your meditation to a place where there is no thought. Go into the empty space where time dissolves. Go into the void. Feel the vibration of the universe. Feel the universal energy move through you. Feel the radiance of your own energy field. Reside in that space of stillness and feel with your whole being the serenity in your meditation.

Early Morning

Have you ever felt the serenity in the early morning? Have you ever felt the pure bliss in the early hours before dawn? Let the silence in the early morning take you deeper into stillness. Let it take you deeper into being. Feel the pure joy in that silence. Let yourself be mesmerized by the beauty of the dark sky filled with stars. Feel the morning breeze as you open the window. There is a deep silence in the morning before dawn. There is deep peace and serenity concealed within it. Let it take you into stillness. Let it take you into joy.

Pure Souls

We are pure souls walking on the planet, looking for our purpose; looking for our mission. We descend from the sky, from the world beyond, onto earth, and forget who we are. We are infinite spiritual beings appearing in human form for a little while and returning once more to the infinite realm. We seek only to understand ourselves. We seek only to know who we really are. We walk on our journey searching for truth. We are on a search for where we came from. What we seek is self-realization.

In our search, we are each unfolding our own story. We are each experiencing life in different ways. We are beings of infinite potential. We are pure souls who have forgotten who we are.

Divine Beings

You are the universe expressing itself in human form. The universe is experiencing itself through you; through your existence. The essence of the universe is pure love and joy and it wants to experience that through you. Realize deeply that you are not separate from the universe. You are one with it. You are interconnected with everything in the cosmos. You are one with everything in existence. You are the source of abundance. You are the source of joy. You are here to allow the mystery of life to unfold. You are here so life can live through you. You are a divine being walking on the planet, mistakenly assuming you are merely a human. Come and return to the root of your own soul. Recognize your own divinity.

Stay Centered

No matter what circumstance you find yourself in, always retain your peace. Always keep your inner stillness. If you happen to be in the midst of negativity and chaos, visualize a protective aura around you and remain centered. Remain grounded. Stay in this protective space and don't allow any negativity in. Don't engage in drama, argument, gossip, or negativity in any form. Retain your space. Dwell in your own space. Train your mind to remain still. Go deeper within. Feel your own being. Don't allow thought to create a shadow over your joy.

Angels

Some people are pure angels. They come into our lives and show us only kindness. They come and show us the way to a better life. They take us towards the light. They show us how joyful life is meant to be. They show us how to live. They show us that the secret to life is living in a state of love and gratitude. They show us the pure joy of being. Sometimes when we are lost or in the dark, we need someone to show us our own light. Sometimes when we feel disconnected, we need someone to show us the love within our own hearts.

Some people have so much love within their hearts they are able to light the candle in other people's hearts. They are able to light up other people's spirits. They are pure angels.

Creators

We all have creative energy within us. There is an impulse within each of us to create. Within each of us lies the desire to manifest, to bring things into existence. We are joy looking for a way to express. We are always creating in every domain of our life. We are the creators and designers of our own lives. We are all artists. We are creating in every moment, with our thoughts, words, and actions. We create friendships and bonds. We create our character. We create who we are.

If we realize how powerful we are at creating, we become more conscious, more intentional. If we truly recognize our abilities in manifesting, no goal or objective will seem out of reach. We are brilliant creative beings with infinite potential.

Present Moment

Wherever you are and whatever you are doing, be there totally. Whatever task you are engaged in, give it your full attention. Let yourself be absorbed in the present moment. Let yourself dwell in the here and now. Notice that when you are present, you are at peace. There is space. There is stillness inside of you. Feel the joy of being fully alert and aware in the present moment.

The key is in observing and not letting the mind wander; not letting the mind take you away from the beauty of this moment. Living in a state of presence is living in grace. It is the key to liberation.

Treasure

We hold treasure inside of us. If only we knew. Inside of us lies a mine of gold. All the wonders of the world lie at the depth of our spirit. Everything we want is already within us. Everything we want to be, we already are.

So often, we look for things outside of us. So often we go after love, beauty, and joy, not realizing all those things are a part of who we are. They are part of our innermost being. If only we knew what we have inside us, we wouldn't be looking to the outside world. We would only look within. If only we knew, we would seek to discover our own depth. We would seek to discover our own being. At the core of our soul, at the depth of our being, lies the greatest treasure.

Beings of Light

We are beings of light. We hold the light within our heart. We hold the light deep within our soul. We are the universe made manifest. We are the universe expressing itself. We are creatures of infinite talent. We come from another realm. We are on a journey of love. Our mission is to express and share our love with the world. Our purpose is to bring our light and love into this dimension. We are cosmic beings in a vast ocean of universal energy. We are multidimensional beings, both earthly and other-worldly. All we have to do is recognize our own depth, our own limitlessness. We hold infinite love within us that we long to share—that we long to express.

Soul Food

Just as the body needs food, so too does the soul. The soul is nourished by love and kindness. By loving ourselves, by doing things for our soul, we nourish it. By spending time with those we love and cherish, we revitalize our soul's energy. By meditating and going into stillness, we allow the soul to rest. The soul is here for its own joy. It wants to express its joy through experience. The soul seeks self-expression. By experiencing the wonders of life, by doing things out of love, by manifesting its desires, the soul expresses its own joy. By bringing love, joy, and beauty into this world, the soul experiences itself. These are food for the soul.

Fear

Fear is only an illusion. We think it's necessary until we realize it is unnecessary. Fear is the opposite of faith. It is a lack of trust within the heart. It's when we doubt our own abilities or the powers of the universe.

Whenever we notice we are falling into fear, we have to pull ourselves out of it. We have to bring ourselves back to the present moment and realize that fear lacks purpose. It doesn't serve us. Only trusting, believing, and persevering serve us on our journey.

Fear is simply made by the mind. It is ultimately fictitious. Faith resides in the heart. It is a deep sense of connectedness. It is trusting in the unseen. Fear pulls us back. It makes us stagnate. Faith helps us move forward. It helps us grow. Fear is a sense of disconnection from life. Faith is a sense of unity with life. Fear has a low vibrational frequency whereas faith has a high vibrational frequency. We have to observe our mind and let go of any fear or doubt that we may hold. We only have to believe.

Pain

Sometimes we go through so much pain and we can't understand what the purpose of it is or why pain and suffering exist. Sometimes we can't conceive of how life works. But we have to realize that pain does have a purpose. It makes us more empathetic. It allows us to understand and connect with people on a deeper level. Without the pain and suffering we've gone through, there would be no depth to us as humans. There would be no humility or compassion in us. There would be no compassion in us. Pain and suffering often crack the shell of the ego and allow our deeper self, our soul, to emerge. Through compassion, we can use our pain as our greatest strength, our greatest asset. We can use it for self-transformation. We can use it to help lessen the suffering of others. We can use it to create change for the better.

Believe

If there is something you want to achieve, you must first believe in yourself. Believe in your own powers and abilities. Close your eyes and feel a deep trust within your heart. Believe that whatever you put your mind and heart into, you can achieve. Believe that whatever it is you desire deep down, you can manifest.

If there is something that lights up your spirit, that makes you ecstatic, that brings you deep joy, pursue it with your whole being. If there's something that creates a spark within your heart, go after it fearlessly. Even if you don't know how to get there, even if you don't have the complete map, just trust. Take the first step and start the journey towards your dream. Everything will fall into place of its own accord. Just rest your heart and believe.

Wish

If you have a wish, send it out into the universe. Free it from personal will. Let it roam free and light in its own desire. Don't worry about the outcome. Everything we want already lies within the Unmanifest, the realm of possibilities. Don't worry about how it will manifest. The universe will find a way to bring it into existence. The universe is intelligent. It has ways beyond our understanding, beyond what our mind can conceive. Don't worry about how or when your wish will come true. Just trust the process. Know that when you want something from your heart, the entire universe conspires in helping you achieve it. Make a wish. Release it. Let go of the outcome. Trust.

Heart and Mind

You must make a bridge between your heart and your mind. You must connect the two so they work effectively together. You have to ask your heart for direction and your mind for wisdom. You have to find what you want from deep within yourself and find a way to reach it. Neither heart nor mind alone will suffice in helping you achieve your desire. Neither one can work effectively without the other.

You can't rely either on your heart or your mind, for each is incomplete. Each has its downfalls. If you rely only on your mind, you will find your life devoid of vibrancy and your decisions without any energy behind them. You won't feel joy from within. You won't know what your soul wants.

On the other hand, if you rely solely on your heart, your decisions will become purely emotional. You will become a dreamer who does not weigh the consequences of their actions. You may become someone who makes rash decisions. You will lack the guidance in your choices, or may not know how to work around obstacles.

Hence, you need to build this bridge. You have to create a communion between your heart and your mind, a pathway for them to communicate so they can work together in harmony; so you may go after what your heart wants and use your mind to create a strategy and work through challenges. So your decisions come from the depth of your being and are also wise. So you live a balanced and harmonious life.

Your heart and mind must come together.

Soul Tribe

Surround yourself with those who support your growth. Surround yourself with those who help you live deeper in the spirit—those who tell you to follow your heart. Don't stay long with those who bring you down. Don't spend time with those who dim your light and make your heart feel heavy. Be with those who light the candle of your spirit, those who help you shine. Be with those who celebrate your success. They are your soul tribe; the people who stand beside you in all circumstances. The people who pull you up. The ones who rejoice in your success and see your growth as their own growth. The ones who see you as themselves and give you a sense of unity. The ones who are with you in heart and spirit.

Find your soul tribe and share the love and the light in your heart with them.

                    SARA BIGHASH

Wisdom of Uncertainty

Sometimes when we want to create change in our lives or take a new course of action, we start having fear and doubt. We start fearing the unknown. We cannot know for sure what the end result of our actions will be or where it may lead, and this uncertainty scares us at times. Sometimes we want to be able to see where something will lead; we want to see what lies ahead. But it just isn't possible. We cannot always know for sure, nor can we control the outcome. But there is wisdom in uncertainty. There is beauty in not knowing. We learn to trust our heart and let it guide us. We learn to welcome change rather than be afraid of it. We learn to internally accept whatever may happen and let go of the illusion of control. We learn to find peace in not knowing and make friends with the unknown. We let life take the lead and steer us in the direction it wants. We learn to trust the process and not worry about the outcome. We allow uncertainty to instill its wisdom in us.

Hero

Be your own hero. Save yourself from negativity. Reclaim your power. Free yourself from anything that is pulling you down, anything that does not serve you. Let go of doubt, blame, and jealousy, and live from a place of love. Let judgement, hate, anger, envy, and sadness fade away from your life and open up space for joy to grow.

Save yourself from negative thoughts that may come your way. Stay alert and aware, and don't let your mind wander into darkness. Come back to yourself, your own presence. Remain inside your own joy, your own bliss. Save yourself from limiting beliefs that are holding you back and follow your spirit. Break your own boundaries, your own limitations, by stepping out of your comfort zone and into the unknown. Challenge yourself to give your all every day. Transcend your own fears and doubts. Rise above. Be your own hero.

Stillness

Take a day off from the clamor. Dive into silence. Let your soul reside in stillness. Feel your inner being. Feel the intensity of your own presence. Allow your soul to rest. Revitalize your energy. Take time for yourself. Get away from routine, from habit. Dwell in your own presence. Feel the aliveness of your inner body. Look at life from a deeper perspective. Listen to the guidance of your soul. Trust your intuition.

Listen to silence. It has much to tell you.

Free like a Bird

Have you ever noticed a bird singing by itself? Have you ever felt drawn to the freedom of the bird, who doesn't care who's listening and only sings for its own joy? We too can be like a bird, doing what makes our soul happy, without worrying about an audience; not concerning ourselves with who is listening. When we do things from our soul, we feel a river of joy within us. We feel liberated. When we do things for ourselves and not to please or impress others, we obtain ultimate freedom.

Do what makes your soul dance. Don't worry about how others will perceive you. Don't worry about your self-image. Free yourself. Liberate your soul.

The Mystic

The mystic is one who embarks on the spiritual journey in search for truth. The mystic is always on the path, never arriving. For the mystic, the path is a destination itself. The journey is an end in and of itself. The mystic is not after theology or ideology. She is after the experience of truth, the experience of self-realization. The mystic doesn't concern himself with the things of this world but seeks to uncover the mysteries of the universe. For the mystic, the ultimate objective is the felt oneness with all, a felt oneness with the divine. The mystic seeks to understand the language of the soul and the algorithm of the universe. The mystic is always a seeker.

Your Journey

Your journey in life is only yours. It belongs to no one else but you. You are here to grow and become the best version of yourself. You are here to grow into the most beautiful and wonderful version of you. Don't compare yourself to anyone else. Don't compare your growth with anyone else's growth. You are not walking on their journey and they're not walking on yours. You have your own mission in life, your own divine purpose.

Be inspired by others and learn from them, but don't measure your progress against them. Seek help from others along your journey but know that ultimately, it is your journey and you are the one walking it. Put all of your focus on your path and don't concern yourself with how far others have gone compared to you. Only seek to improve yourself. Only seek to better yourself. Compare your progress only with yourself. We are each here on our own journey.

Imagination

Imagination is a powerful tool. It is the creative faculty of the mind. Mind and logic can take you many places, but imagination takes you everywhere. It takes you where the mind cannot. It takes you beyond this world. With your imagination, you can explore the unknown. You can transcend any limitation. With your imagination, you can experience anything. With your imagination, you can go beyond what you thought was possible. You can come up with new solutions. You can bring new things into existence that were previously unthought of. You can tap into your creative potential and think outside the box. With imagination, you are able to see beyond what the mind can see.

Imagination takes you into the realm of infinite possibilities. Use the power of your imagination to bring creative energy into your life. Use your imagination to go beyond this world.

Open Your Heart

This life has so much to offer. This life is so filled with love. If you open your heart, you'll see all the love and beauty in this life. If you open your heart, you'll see goodness all around you. Life itself is a miracle, giving to us in abundance, opening doors of opportunity for us. If we open our hearts, there is so much loving and healing energy available to us in every moment. If we open our hearts, we will see the wonders of the world. We will get a glimpse of the secrets of the universe. We will begin to realize how beautiful life truly is. We will feel a deep peace within our hearts.

Open your heart and allow life to shower you with love. Open your heart and receive all the love and joy life has to offer.

Breathe

Whenever you feel like you're drifting into thought or you feel out of alignment, just breathe. Let your breath anchor you in the present moment. Let it take you into stillness. Allow the breath to calm your mind and bring you back to the here and now.

Our life is in the breath. By creating harmony in our breath, we create harmony in our mind and in our life. By breathing consciously, we go deeper into awareness. Breathe in deeply and feel oxygen fill your lungs. Feel life flowing through you. Feel the serenity in your breath. Just breathe.

Dance of Life

Life is the dance and you are the dancer. Life is experiencing itself through you. Life is living through you. Allow life to flow through you and express itself. Let life sway you in the direction it wants and show you its wonders. Let life dance through you. Let life sweep you off your feet. Let go of resistance and let the pure energy of life flow through you. Let it exult your spirit and lift you. Feel the force of life with your entire being. Always say yes to life. Open yourself to all life has to give. Let life set you free. Let life itself liberate you. Participate and enjoy the dance of life.

The Heart

The heart is the seat of the soul. It's where our divinity originates. It is the fourth center of our energetic body, connecting the physical and the spiritual realm. Through the heart, we can make decisions based on our higher self. Through love and compassion, we can bring our spiritual nature into this world. The heart is our gateway to spiritual ascension. The deeper we go into the heart, the closer we are to the spirit. The heart allows us to follow the light and transcend our earthly concerns. Through the heart, we find depth within ourselves. Through the heart, we are able to see what lies beyond appearances. We're able to read energies and intentions. Through the heart, we're able to know from within, to intuit. Through the vibration of the heart we're able to connect with others on an energetic level. The heart allows us to follow our soul's desires and make our dreams come true.

Abracadabra

The term *abracadabra* comes from the Aramaic phrase *avra kehdabra,* which means, "I will create as I speak." The words we speak are powerful. Speaking has a vibration. There is energy behind everything we say. Each word and each sentence has a frequency and sends a message out into the universe. The words we speak have great creative power.

By feeling and believing the words we speak, we manifest. With the power of the spoken word, we bring things into existence. Be wise in your choice of words. Be wise in how you speak. Your words have the potential to create. They draw you closer to what you are saying, like a magnet. Become conscious of what you believe, think, and say. Choose to focus on your wishes. Focus your attention and energy on your deepest desires. With the power of your intention, attention, and belief, you can speak things into existence. Believe in your heart that your wishes can manifest. Say abracadabra and make your dreams come true.

Three Principles

Never judge a situation, for you don't know if it's truly good or bad. A seemingly positive situation can turn into a negative one. A seemingly misfortunate event can turn out to be in your favor.

Never attach yourself to anything. Not a person, an object, or an identity. Everything in the world of form is inherently unstable, always changing by nature. Don't seek to find yourself in any of the things in the physical realm. Live free from attachment. Never resist anything that comes your way. Resisting a situation is resisting life, and negativity arises out of that. Let go of what you cannot control and allow everything to be. Let every situation pass. Always internally accept what is, before you act. Operate from a place of inner peace. Non-judgement, non-attachment, and non-resistance are three principles that, if implemented, lead to happiness.

Leader

Be the leader of your own life. Pave your own path and guide yourself through obstacles. Find the light within your own heart and let it show you the way. Follow the guidance of your soul. In times of difficulty, seek the strength within yourself. When confronted with challenges, find courage in your own heart and spirit. Lead yourself in the direction of your soul and find your inner purpose. Walk through life fearlessly and pursue what it is that you want deep down. Manifest your deepest desires. Seek wisdom from your higher self and when in doubt, ask your heart. Unfold your own story and create your own destiny. Be the leader of your own life.

Creativity

Creativity is the soul's urge to create through us. It is the soul expressing its own beauty, its own depth through us. Creativity is born out of the stillness of the mind. It's when we go beyond the mind that creativity arises. It's when we go deep within ourselves that we find the spark. Creativity is the soul bringing the creative force of the universe into manifestation. It is the soul participating in the creative urge of the universe.

We are infinite, creative geniuses looking for a way to express. Become a conscious participant in the creative process and allow for the creative impulse of the universe to express itself through you. Go deeper within and allow your creativity to rise.

Law of Attraction

Be mindful of your self-talk. It's a conversation with the universe. You are always communicating with the universe whether you realize it or not. Every thought you think, every emotion you feel, and every action you take has a certain vibrational frequency. You are always sending vibes out into the universe. The universe is always picking up on how you are being.

Your inner state is the energy you bring into whatever you do. If you are in a state of peace, love and gratitude, you bring that energy into what you do. Similarly, if you are in a state of frustration or resistance, that is the energy you are operating from. Always pay attention to your internal state. The universe is always listening and responding with similar energy. Like attracts like. Always retain your peace of mind and operate from stillness. Whenever you notice a negative state arising, recognize it and give it space to dissolve. Be mindful of how you are being and what you are attracting. The universe is always listening.

Magnet

Become a magnet. Engineer yourself in such a way that everything you want comes to you. You don't have to chase anything. Create such joy within yourself that all joyful things come your way. Raise your vibration so high that you attract positivity wherever you go. Radiate such light that all the good in this world comes to you. Look into the depths of your soul and allow the goodness you have within to emerge. Go into stillness and nurture the seeds of love and gratitude within yourself. You are a being of energy. Like a magnet, you attract what you are. Radiate love and positivity out into the world and watch as it returns to you. Watch how magic happens.

Grateful

Wake up each morning with a grateful heart. Be thankful for this new day you are given. Feel the pure joy of life itself. Close your eyes, put your hand on your heart, and feel your heartbeat. Feel the vibration of your heart. Feel the vibration of love. Give thanks to your heart for beating for you, for keeping you alive. Feel the energy field of your own being. Feel your inner body. Your ethereal body. Your light body. Feel your own vibrancy from deep within. Give thanks to the universe for infusing its own energy within you, for creating you out of the Unmanifest. Give thanks for life itself, for life is the greatest gift we have.

Deeper Connections

As we grow on our spiritual journey, we seek deeper connections. We are no longer satisfied with superficial relationships. We no longer seek to be with others to pass the time or avoid feeling lonely. We seek out true friendships that are grounded in love, trust, and understanding. We seek those who understand us, those that see through to our heart. We seek those we connect with on a spiritual level, those who understand our soul. We seek those with whom we can form a deep sense of trust; those with whom we can share what is in our heart. We seek those that help our spiritual growth, those who help us become better versions of ourselves. As we grow, some friendships dissolve, others strengthen, and new ones arise.

Adversity

Sometimes when adversity strikes, it can make us realize what's truly important in life. Sometimes when things seem to fall apart, it can cause a shift to happen within us; a shift in our perspective. It can make us rearrange our priorities in an instant. It can make us realize what is worthy of our time and attention and what is not. It gives us a new lens through which to see life. It removes the veil of illusion and makes us see things more clearly.

Many of the things we thought were important suddenly lose their significance. Our attention gets redirected towards what truly matters. We start cherishing the valuable things in life and letting go of unnecessary baggage. We realize that love and kindness is all that matters. We start appreciating the people in our life more and realize that nothing lasts except the love and compassion within our hearts. Adversity can be a great teacher and give us spiritual clarity. Adversity is often a blessing in disguise.

Child Within

There's a child within you that seeks your attention. A child within you longs to play and express itself. Hold that child in your loving embrace. Treat that child with love and kindness. Allow the child within to bring deep joy into your life. Allow the child within to roam free and explore the world. Allow yourself to look at the world through the eyes of the child within, looking at everything with awe and curiosity, finding joy in the simplest things. Allow the child within to come out by immersing yourself in creative activity, by doing things for the sheer joy of it. By doing things that light up your spirit.

Don't let age extinguish the joy of the child inside of you. Recognize the child within you and let it express itself. Be free like the child within you.

New Journey

Have you ever decided to embark on a journey? Have you ever decided to start a new path? When we go on a new journey, we are starting a new adventure, a new story. We're opening a new door for ourselves and seeking new experiences. We're allowing new energy to enter our life. Sometimes all it takes is one decision to turn our life upside down. Sometimes all it takes is one choice to change the direction of our life completely. Sometimes, by taking a leap of faith, we change the course of our life and go beyond our own fears and limitations. We go beyond what we thought was possible.

You have to open your mind to go beyond your own limits. You have to open your heart to allow new experiences to enter your life. Dare to start a new journey in your life and discover what life has to offer.

Ocean

Life is an ocean and you are a wave. You are not separate from life. You are one with it. Though you may think you are on your own, in truth, you are always connected to the whole. You are Source made manifest. You are one with the energy that is sustaining life. Though you have your individual journey, you are also part of the collective. Always remember that you are not just a wave. You are as vast and deep as the ocean itself.

Tunnel Vision

When you truly want something, when you have a goal, a vision, put all of your focus towards it. Use tunnel vision and avoid distractions. By focusing on your goal, anything that doesn't serve you fades away and the light of your intention becomes stronger. By using tunnel vision, you don't allow anything to take your attention away from your goal. You channel your energy in the direction you want. You find strength and discipline within yourself. Your focus becomes sharp, and you pursue your deepest desires without fear. Focus your attention on your vision and follow your dreams. Don't let anything stop you.

The Sun

The sun is powerful. It radiates energy to the earth and the cosmos. What if I told you that you too can be like the sun? You are a radiant being with the power to light up other people's spirits and hearts with your kind words and gestures. You can create a spark inside other people by radiating your love to everyone around you. By becoming aware of the light within your heart and setting the intention to spread it to others, you too can be like the sun. You too can radiate light.

Recognize your own power. Recognize the goodness you hold within you. Realize that you are a being of light and set the intention to give light. Become like a sun and give your love and kindness to everyone around you.

Bravery

Bravery comes from looking at the darkness within ourselves and transmuting it into light. Bravery comes from letting go of our own assumptions and changing our beliefs in the face of new experiences. Bravery is when we can honestly look into our own mistakes and learn from them. It's when we can openly admit that we may have been wrong and seek to change our ways. It's when we are willing to adapt.

Bravery is when we follow our heart and go after our dreams without fear. It's when we transcend our fear and follow our spirit. Bravery comes from doing the right thing even though it may hurt, even if it may result in loss. Bravery comes from going beyond our limitations and living in the heart.

Guru

The word *guru* consists of two parts: "Gu" meaning darkness, and "Ru" meaning light. A guru is one who takes you out of the darkness and into the light. A guru is someone who removes the veil of illusion and helps you see things clearly, one who helps you tap into your inner strengths and find the light within your heart. She is one who gives you courage in your darkest times; one who opens your heart to the universe. He is one who guides you along your path and leads you in the right direction, one who brings to the surface your shadows so that with the light of your awareness, you can transmute them. She tells you where your strengths are and what you need to work on.

A guru is one who helps you ascend to your higher self; one who believes in you wholeheartedly and with that, enables you to believe in yourself. A guru helps you journey within yourself and discover the depth of your own soul.

Inner Work

Inner work means turning inwards and facing our own shadows. It's when we openly and consciously look at our deepest pains and seek to heal them with the light of our consciousness. It's when we look honestly at our own shortcomings and seek to improve them with our awareness. Inner work means having the courage to bring the darkness within us out of the shadows and into the light. Inner work means seeking to heal ourselves first rather than fixing outside circumstances. It's a process of inward reflection, self-love, and healing. Inner work means recreating ourselves. It means engineering ourselves in a way that we become a magnet for our dreams. Inner work is when we seek to perform alchemy and turn our greatest pains into our greatest powers. Inner work means seeking to transcend who we are and reach our higher selves.

Guides

If we pay attention, everyone we meet along our path is our guide. Each person we meet teaches us something. Each person is either directly or indirectly telling us how to be and how not to be. Each person exhibits an array of behaviors and characteristics. Based on the feeling we get from what we see, we intuitively know which behaviors we want to adopt and which ones we want to avoid. We learn from the actions and attitudes of others. We can consciously choose who we want to be by watching others. We have the power and the freedom to design ourselves the way we want. We are able to use the guidance of others in shaping who we wish to become. Everyone around us is our guide.

Who We Are

We hold within us all the wonders of the world. We hold within us all the knowledge and wisdom of the universe. At the depth of our being, we know who we are and where we came from. Deep within our soul, we always know what we want. No knowledge lies outside of us. There is no truth that, deep down, we don't already know. We have simply forgotten.

We are on a journey here on earth to remember who we really are. We are here to rediscover the depth of our own being. We are here to relearn the secrets of our soul.

Although we appear in physical form, who we are is beyond the physical realm. Who we are is beyond the dimension of time and space. We are beings of the universe, made of pure light. This life is a temporary play of forms, a place where we get to experience and express ourselves. It's where we remember who we really are. We are only temporarily human. Our souls are infinite, like the universe.

At the age of 22, Sara Bighash experienced an internal shift that changed her state of being. This inner shift created a sense of stillness within her that caused her to perceive life differently. Drawn towards various spiritual teachings and meditation practices, she saw this change reflected in her everyday life and personal relationships.

While in university, Sara began to journal as a form of connecting with her inner self and self-expression. Her writing was predominantly geared towards spirituality and self-reflections and from her journals, the idea of this book was born. Through her writing, she intends to inspire readers to live from the heart, connect with their inner self, and follow their soul's guidance.